D1483700

Lighting the World

BOOK 2, ACTS 9—15

The
ACTS
of the
HOLY
SPIRIT
Series

BOOK
2

Lighting the World

A NEW LOOK AT ACTS —
GOD'S HANDBOOK FOR
WORLD EVANGELISM

C. PETER WAGNER

Regal Books
A Division of Gospel Light
Ventura, California, U.S.A.

Published by Regal Books
A Division of Gospel Light
Ventura, California, U.S.A.
Printed in U.S.A.

Regal Books is a ministry of Gospel Light, an evangelical Christian publisher dedicated to serving the local church. We believe God's vision for Gospel Light is to provide church leaders with biblical, user-friendly materials that will help them evangelize, disciple and minister to children, youth and families.

It is our prayer that this Regal Book will help you discover biblical truth for your own life and help you meet the needs of others. May God richly bless you.

For a free catalog of resources from Regal Books/Gospel Light please contact your Christian supplier or call 1-800-4-GOSPEL.

Scripture quotations in this publication are from *The New King James Version*. Copyright © 1979, 1980, 1982, Thomas Nelson, Inc. Used by permission.

This book is also available in Spanish (ISBN 1-56063-847-8) and Portuguese (1-56063-943-1). Published by Editorial Unilit, Miami, Florida.

Library of Congress Cataloging-in-Publication Data
Wagner, C. Peter.
    The Acts of the Holy Spirit series.

    Contents: v. 1. Spreading the fire : Acts 1-8 — v. 2. Lighting the world.
    1. Bible. N.T. Acts—Commentaries. I. Title.
BS2625.3.W35   1994   226.6'07   94-30400
ISBN 0-8307-1710-2 (v. 1)H.C.
ISBN 0-8307-1718-8 (v. 2)H.C.

1 2 3 4 5 6 7 8 9 10 11 12 13 14 /KP/ 02 01 99 98 97 96 95

Rights for publishing this book in other languages are contracted by Gospel Literature International (GLINT). GLINT also provides technical help for the adaptation, translation and publishing of Bible study resources and books in scores of languages worldwide. For further information, contact GLINT, P.O. Box 4060, Ontario, CA 91761-1003, U.S.A., or the publisher.

Contents

1. Meet Paul—The Greatest Missionary of All Time: Acts 9   17

"The Lord's commission to Paul combines the two major themes of the Acts of the Apostles: missiology and power ministries."

2. Peter Blazes the Trail to the Gentiles: Acts 9, 10 and 11   53

"God had anointed Peter as the apostle to the circumcision, but when called upon to break the Gentile barrier in the house of Cornelius, he rose to the occasion, ministered to the uncircumcision and turned a key to the Kingdom that has seen multiplied benefits through the centuries."

3. Planting the First Gentile Church: Acts 11   87

"The city of Antioch, from this point in history, begins to rise in importance as the center of early Christianity on a par with Jerusalem. It is the place where the first Gentile church, in the proper sense of the word, was to be established."

Introduction to the Acts Series

This commentary on the book of Acts is my first attempt at a verse-by-verse exposition of a book of the Bible. It may be the last. As a field missionary and a professional missiologist, I have been consumed by the Acts of the Apostles, which I regard as a kind of owner's manual for implementing the Great Commission. I have studied and taught Acts more than any other book.

The full rationale for choosing to undertake this massive project is so crucial to understanding Acts as a whole, that I began the first book of this series with a whole chapter to explain it.

Because I am not known in the academic world as a biblical scholar, I have asked my friend Professor Russell P. Spittler, who is so known, to peruse the manuscripts previous to publication and to monitor the technical elements of biblical scholarship that appear from time to time. This does not imply Dr. Spittler's personal endorsement of each of my *interpretations* of the biblical text. Many of the themes I discuss fall clearly into areas of contemporary theological dialogue and even controversy. So many of them do, in fact, that it may be no reader at all will end up agreeing with everything I say!

Be that as it may, I am deeply indebted to Russ Spittler for his wise and knowledgeable counsel, as well as to the several authors of standard commentaries on Acts whom I frequently quote.

C. Peter Wagner
Fuller Theological Seminary
Pasadena, California

···

Introduction to This Book

Some who are reading this book will have read Book 1 of this three-volume teaching on Acts, *Spreading the Fire*. Others are just starting at this point, and it is especially for them I am offering this introduction.

First, I will explain why I am writing a commentary on the book of Acts. Second, I will summarize the high points of what I consider notably important through the first eight chapters of Acts.

Why Another Commentary?

According to a recent computer search, 1,398 commentaries on Acts are currently available. Why, then, commentary number 1,399?

I have been teaching the Acts of the Apostles for almost 15 years, and I have built a substantial library of commentaries dealing with this book. The commentaries are excellent and well respected among preachers, teachers and biblical scholars. It has become evident to me, however, that the existing literature contains two general areas of weakness. Let me explain.

Virtually all the commentaries point out that Acts 1:8 serves as an outline of what Luke will be dealing with in the 28 chapters of the book of Acts:

···

But you shall receive power when the Holy Spirit
has come upon you; and you shall be witnesses to Me
in Jerusalem, and in all Judea and Samaria, and to
the end of the earth (1:8).

···

This text, quite plainly, has two emphases: (1) supernatural power, and (2) cross-cultural missions. Interestingly enough, these are the two most evident areas of weakness in the standard commentaries. By this I do not mean that the classical authors fail to mention these things, but most do so only in passing. Very few have specialized in either of them to any significant degree in their professional ministries, and none whom I have found so far has specialized in both. I, therefore, believe I can make a contribution with commentary number 1,399 because I have been a professional missiologist since 1971, and I have taken a place of leadership both nationally and internationally in areas of power ministries since 1982.

This by no means makes any other commentary obsolete. Each author I am consulting has unique contributions to our total knowledge of the book of Acts, which I regard as a training manual for modern Christians. I would not be able to write this commentary without standing on the shoulders of the dedicated and creative scholars who have gone before. I highly recommend several other commentaries, especially those written by F. F. Bruce, Simon Kistemaker and John Stott. These references, and others, appear in my endnotes.

A phenomenon that seems to lend special urgency to a new commentary of this nature is the veritable explosion of knowledge in the fields of missiology and power ministries over the last two decades or so. As late as 1970, missiology was not recognized as an academic field in the United States. It is now well established. In the 1980s, controversies were raging around the validity of power ministries such as signs and wonders, demonic deliverance and spiritual warfare. In some circles debate continues, but it has cooled down considerably. Prior to 1980, however, supernatural power was hardly a chief topic of discussion among those of us who were not Pentecostals or charismatics.

It is not surprising, therefore, that our classic commentators of the past would not have dealt with these rapidly expanding areas in the depth it is possible to do today.

Highlights of Acts 1—8

The book of Acts begins with a group of 120 people from a narrow slice of the demographic pie of the first-century Roman Empire.

For a starter, all the believers were Jews. No Gentiles, or Samaritans—who were half Jewish—were among them. Not only that, the believers were Hebrew Jews, residents of Palestine, as opposed to Hellenistic Jews who lived in other parts of the Roman Empire. Furthermore, the group was not made up of the more sophisticated Judean Hebrew Jews, but rather the backwoods Galilean Hebrew Jews from the north, roughly equivalent to what we might describe today as "hillbillies." Not surprisingly, this was the same ethnic group Jesus Himself belonged to—Aramaic-speaking Galilean Jews.

This background is important for understanding the missiology of the book of Acts. The first cross-cultural ministry is seen in Acts 2 when, on the Day of Pentecost, large numbers of Hellenistic Jews also became followers of Jesus. As the church grew from 120 to 3,000, then to 15,000 and more, a problem surfaced that is seen sooner or later on virtually every mission field in the world. The church contains two significant people groups, in this case Hebrews and Hellenists, but the leadership is in the hands of only one group here in Jerusalem, the Hebrews. The Hellenists, although they were possibly a numerical majority by the time of the events in Acts 6, thought they were being discriminated against by the Hebrews and their widows were not being treated fairly.

The upshot was that the church divided along cultural lines, the apostles remaining in leadership of the Hebrew segment and seven Hellenistic disciples taking the leadership of the Hellenistic segment. I am aware that some may say this is not the usual interpretation of what happened, but *Spreading the Fire* contains substantial material for those who wish to explore it in more depth. Among other things, when the persecution came against the church following Stephen's death, the believers were driven from the city of Jerusalem **except the apostles** (8:1). Many commentators, me included, take this to mean that the Hellenists were scattered, but not the Hebrews. The division in the church was by then recognized even by the persecutors.

Part of the evangelistic significance of this division will reappear when we come to Acts 11 later in this book: **Now those who were scattered after the persecution that arose over Stephen traveled as far as Phoenicia, Cyprus, and Antioch, preaching the word to no one but the Jews only (v. 19).**

A much more radical challenge came immediately when Philip, who was one of the seven Hellenistic leaders driven from Jerusalem, found himself in the midst of the much-despised Samaritans. The crucial missiological question then became: If Samaritans wish to accept Jesus as their Messiah, do they first have to become Jews? Philip's opinion—and the opinion of Peter and John, who later went to Samaria to check it out—was that they did not have to first become Jews, but rather they could be considered Messianic Samaritans. This conformed with the brilliant discourse of Stephen, recorded in Acts 7, which offended the unbelieving Jews so much it cost Stephen his life. The missiological importance of this sequence of events is, in my opinion, on a par equal to that of the Council of Jerusalem, which we will study in detail when we come to Acts 15.

These are the missiological highlights of *Spreading the Fire*. Now let me mention those highlights relating to power ministries.

Power Ministries in Acts 1—8

It took only 10 days for Jesus' promise of power in Acts 1:8 to materialize. On the Day of Pentecost, the disciples were involved in a miraculous event that was different from anything Jesus Himself ever did: They shared the gospel in 15 languages they had never learned! Three thousand people were saved as a consequence.

Following **many wonders and signs...done through the apostles** (2:43), Peter and John healed a lame man at the Temple and the number of disciples grew to 5,000 men, conservatively a total of 15,000 people (see 4:4).

Later, **great fear came upon all the church** (5:11) when God manifested His power in taking life from the hypocrites Ananias and Sapphira (see 5:1-11). Shortly afterward, so much divine power was released that Peter's shadow itself healed the sick and demons were being cast out. And an angelic visitation released the apostles from prison. Lest we think power ministries were confined to the 12 apostles, Stephen also **did great wonders and signs among the people** (6:8), and multitudes were saved under Philip's ministry upon **hearing and seeing the miracles which he did** (8:6). Neither Stephen nor Philip were among the 12.

A significant power encounter occurred when Simon the Sorcerer, considered by the Samaritans **the great power of God** (8:10), tried to buy supernatural power from the apostles with money. This was a prototype of several incidents of spiritual warfare that are yet to come in our study of Acts. An amazing case of spiritual transport is later recorded when, after he baptized the Ethiopian eunuch, **the Spirit of the Lord caught Philip away, so that the eunuch saw him no more** (8:39).

The implications for the spread of the gospel that these clear examples of power ministries have for missionary work in our own day are awesome. I believe we are living in what may well be the years of the final thrust of world evangelization. Although some may question such a sweeping statement, I believe I have evidence to show that virtually everything we read about in the book of Acts is being reported from many parts of the world today, and the frequency and drama of such tangible manifestations of God's power seem to be increasing almost daily.

We have much more to learn as we pick up Luke's flow of events in Acts 9.

A Time Line
of Acts

Not all scholars agree on the dates for the sequence of events in the book of Acts. Although the matter has been thoroughly researched by competent specialists, consensus has not yet been attained. I do not care to repeat the arguments for different time lines, which are readily accessible in the various critical commentaries, but it is necessary to form an opinion. Here are some of the chief dates and events I am adopting (all dates are A.D.):

30	Pentecost
31	Persecution from fellow Jews becomes severe
32	The gospel moves from the Hebrews to the Jewish Hellenists
	Philip evangelizes Samaria
	The gospel enters North Africa
33	Saul is converted, travels to Jerusalem
34-36	Paul in Damascus, Arabia, Jerusalem
	Peter evangelizes Judea
37-45	Paul in Cilicia and Syria
	Peter continues in Judea
	The missionaries from Cyprus and Cyrene begin to win Gentiles in Antioch
46	Paul goes to Antioch
	James takes leadership of the Jerusalem church
47-48	Paul's first missionary term
49	Paul's furlough
	The Jerusalem Council
50-52	Paul's second term

CHAPTER

1

Acts 9

Meet Paul—The Greatest Missionary of All Time

Our story of the amazing spread of the gospel through the mighty power of God continues with this shocking description of one of the sworn enemies of Jesus and His followers:

> 1. Then Saul, still breathing threats and murder against the disciples of the Lord, went to the high priest 2. and asked letters from him to the synagogues of Damascus, so that if he found any who were of the Way, whether men or women, he might bring them bound to Jerusalem.

Who was this Saul? It is not farfetched to consider Saul, whose name was later changed to Paul, as the second most significant figure in the history of Christianity next to Jesus Himself. Paul wrote one-fourth of the New Testament. Two-thirds of the book of Acts tells Paul's story. His conversion was so important, it is related three times in Acts. Paul was the principal "bridge of God" from the Jews to the Gentiles, to paraphrase the title of missiologist Donald McGavran's landmark book, *The Bridges of God* (Friendship Press, 1981). Later we will see that Paul was not the first missionary to the Gentiles, but he was certainly the most prominent and was the prototype of all cross-cultural missionaries ever since. Few would call it an exaggeration to label Paul "the greatest missionary of all time."

From a Lion to a Lamb

Before he met Jesus, Paul was a terror. John Stott says it vividly when he writes, "Some of the language Luke uses to describe Paul in his pre-conversion state seems deliberately to portray him as 'a wild and ferocious beast.'"[1] Stott examines the Greek words and cites several scholars who conclude that the language reflects "the ravaging of a body of wild beasts," or "the panting and snorting of wild beasts," and what Paul did to the church was similar to the "mangling by wild beasts, e.g. lions." The lion, by the grace of God, later became a lamb.

Paul was born in Tarsus, a city in what then was Cilicia and what today is Turkey, on the northeast corner of the Mediterranean Sea. Tarsus was a Greek-speaking city, but from this we should not automatically conclude that Paul was a typical Hellenistic Jew. Richard Longenecker says, "It was possible for a thoroughly Hebraic Jew to be born and reared in the Diaspora."[2] The evidence we have points to the more likely conclusion that Paul's principal self-identity was that of a Hebrew as opposed to a Hellenist. He undoubtedly knew Greek, but as a second language, spoken with what we might call today a Yiddish accent. He calls himself a Hebrew born of Hebrews (see Phil. 3:5). Aramaic was his mother tongue, as suggested in the language of Jesus speaking to him on the Damascus road.

Many of the Jews residing in Tarsus, perhaps the majority, would indeed have been Hellenists. They would have been using the *Septuagint*, the Greek translation of the Old Testament, as their Bible and holding their synagogue services in Greek. But, as F. F. Bruce says, "Paul would have been given little opportunity of imbibing the culture of Tarsus during his boyhood: indeed, his parents made sure of an orthodox upbringing for him by arranging for him to spend his formative years in Jerusalem."[3] A modern parallel might be Hasidic Jews in New York City. Although they are citizens of New York City and of the United States of America, they, nevertheless, find their primary social and cultural self-identity as Orthodox Jews. At the same time, the majority of other Jews in New York City are much more Americanized, just as the majority in the first-century Tarsus would likely have been Hellenized.

Paul, therefore, was probably raised in a Jewish ghetto. The word "ghetto" is more broadly used in our days, but through the centuries it usually meant the place where the Jewish community, largely unassimilated, lived in European cities. This fits in with the way Luke reports Paul's public self-description:

> 22:3. "I am indeed a Jew, born in Tarsus of Cilicia, but brought up in this city at the feet of Gamaliel, taught according to the strictness of our fathers' law, and was zealous toward God."

As we saw in Acts 5 when the apostles were brought before the Sanhedrin, Gamaliel was the chief leader of the Pharisees in Jerusalem. Paul greatly values his time studying with Gamaliel, and says later to King Agrippa:

> 26:4. "My manner of life from my youth, which was spent from the beginning among my own nation at

Jerusalem, all the Jews know. 5. ...that according to the
strictest sect of our religion I lived a Pharisee."

....

At another point Paul added, "I am a Pharisee, the son of a
Pharisee" (23:6).

Paul was a full-blooded Jew. He says he was "circumcised the
eighth day, of the stock of Israel, of the tribe of Benjamin" (Phil.
3:5). Not all full-blooded Jews then, as now, were devout practi-
tioners of their faith. Some Jews today are self-declared atheists
or agnostics. Paul, however, was what we might call a "fanatic
Jew." He says, "I advanced in Judaism beyond many of my con-
temporaries in my own nation, being more exceedingly zealous
for the traditions of my fathers" (Gal. 1:14).

I have gone into a good bit of detail on Paul's early background
for two reasons. One, it helps us understand why he might act
like such a wild beast persecuting the believers. Two, because the
essence of missiology is cross-cultural ministry, it is important to
know as clearly as possible what the *cultural* dimensions of Paul's
taking the gospel to the Gentiles ultimately involved.

Some may have noticed that I am citing passages from Acts 22
and Acts 26 along with those from Acts 9 in this section. By way
of explanation, Paul's conversion story appears in all three places,
and in my opinion it will be more helpful if we collate all three in
this chapter instead of postponing mentioning significant bits and
pieces until we come to them in what will be Book 3 of this series.

The Roaring Lion

We are told in the Bible, "Your adversary the devil walks about
like a roaring lion, seeking whom he may devour" (1 Pet. 5:8).
What could better describe Paul, then Saul, walking to Damascus
and **breathing threats and murder against the disciples of the
Lord** (Acts 9:1)?

To understand why Paul was going to Damascus, we must flash back briefly to the story of Stephen in Acts 7 and 8. Stephen was the first theologian of cross-cultural missions. He was an ethnic Jew, but a Hellenist, as opposed to a Hebrew as Paul was. Stephen clearly saw that although the gospel was for Jews, it was also for non-Jews. He saw that salvation through Jesus was not restricted to those who kept the Jewish law and worshiped in the Jerusalem Temple. This naturally irritated the Jewish traditionalists and they recruited false witnesses who said, **"This man does not cease to speak blasphemous words against this holy place and the law"** (6:13). Stephen's subsequent explanation in Acts 7 fanned the flames of their unbelief rather than quenching them and they reacted by murdering Stephen. Luke makes a point of mentioning that Paul was there in person: **And the witnesses laid down their clothes at the feet of a young man named Saul** (7:58).

Paul was diametrically opposed to Stephen's theology of mission at that time. Paul firmly believed that no one could be acceptable to God without becoming a Jew and obeying the law. And because he was a fanatic, as we have seen, he took action:

8:1. Now Saul was consenting to his death.... 3. ...he made havoc of the church, entering every house, and dragging off men and women, committing them to prison.

It is not difficult to feel the emotion here. Here is a man obviously under the power of the enemy who has come to steal, to kill and to destroy. His misdirected zeal has overshadowed any sense of human compassion. This sets the stage for the irony that such a wild beast could later become, of all things, a missionary to the Gentiles, explicitly inviting them to follow Christ without submitting to the Jewish law. Some years later, Paul himself describes this irony to a crowd of Jews in Jerusalem:

22:19-21. "So I said, 'Lord, they know that in every synagogue I imprisoned and beat those who believe on You.
And when the blood of Your martyr Stephen was shed, I
also was standing by consenting to his death, and guarding
the clothes of those who were killing him.' Then He
said to me, 'Depart, for I will send you far from here
to the Gentiles.'"

The reaction of the crowd? They had no liking for what they
heard:

22:22. And they listened to him until this word, and then
they raised their voices and said, "Away with such a fellow from the earth, for he is not fit to live!"

The crowd's desire to kill Paul was exactly how Paul had previously perceived Stephen and the others who had believed in
Jesus as their Messiah! He understood what they were saying.

Heading for Damascus

Paul had become a full-time persecutor of the Messianic Jews. He
had done his best to wipe them out in Judea and Samaria, and perhaps some of the believers from there had escaped to Damascus
when that persecution came. Apparently Paul was not seeking
believers who were natives of Damascus itself, but only those who
had gone there from Jerusalem. His purpose was to arrest them and
to **bring them bound to Jerusalem** (9:2), where the Sanhedrin had
jurisdiction and where they could then be punished.

Paul took with him **letters...to the synagogues of Damascus**
(9:2). We do well to keep in mind that believers were still Jews
in those days and that they naturally continued keeping the

Jewish law and attending their synagogues. No one was yet called a "Christian," and no one would be until the first Gentile churches were firmly established in Antioch. Unfortunately, at least one modern version of the Bible translates the word "disciple" in Acts 9:10 as "Christian," and is, therefore, somewhat misleading.

Rather than "Christian," they are called here those **who were of the Way** (9:2). This is one of the more common terms for first-century believers. For example, in Ephesus later on **there arose a great commotion about the Way** (19:23), and when Paul is defending himself before Felix he explains that he worships God **"according to the Way"** (24:14).

The issue was not whether they were Jews or not. The issue was whether these Messianic Jews were blaspheming God as Stephen had been accused of doing. Paul, with his extremely ethnocentric point of view, thought they were.

The Vision on the Road

9:3. And as he journeyed he came near Damascus, and suddenly a light shone around him from heaven. 4. Then he fell to the ground, and heard a voice saying to him, "Saul, Saul, why are you persecuting Me?" 5. And he said, "Who are You, Lord?" And the Lord said, "I am Jesus, whom you are persecuting. It is hard for you to kick against the goads."

22:6. "Now it happened, as I journeyed and came near Damascus at about noon, suddenly a great light from heaven shone around me. 7. And I fell to the ground and heard a voice saying to me, 'Saul, Saul....'"

26:13. "At midday,...along the road I saw a light from heaven, brighter than the sun, shining around me and

those who journeyed with me. 14. And when we had all
fallen to the ground, I heard a voice speaking to me and
saying in the Hebrew language, 'Saul, Saul....'"

Paul's conversion is one of the more awesome displays of the
power of God in human affairs that we find in Scripture. It
included a supernatural light, a vision, a falling under the power
of the Spirit, hearing the voice of God and a new birth "not of
blood, nor of the will of the flesh, nor of the will of man, but of
God" (John 1:13).

It is hard to imagine being in the Middle East under the
noonday sun, and then being enveloped in a yet brighter light.
We don't know how many others were with Paul on this trip,
but all of them saw the light. I have not personally experienced
such a phenomenon, but several of my friends testify to experiences similar to Paul's. The light here, as in more recent coun-
terparts, is presumably a visible manifestation of the glory
of a holy God. In the transfiguration, it is said that Jesus'
"face shone like the sun, and His clothes became as white as the
light" (Matt. 17:2).

My friend Jack Hayford is one who has experienced seeing the
tangible light of God. In the early days of his pastorate in The
Church On The Way in Van Nuys, California, he had been
struggling with a lethargic congregation and a plateaued membership of about 100 people. Then one Saturday, Jack went into
the sanctuary alone and saw it filled with a silvery mist. He says,
"No earthly dust had the glowing quality that this mist possessed
as it filled the whole room, even where the sunlight was not shining."[4] God had filled the sanctuary with His glory and a church
growth phenomenon began that has reached nearly 10,000 con-
gregants at this writing.

Light dispels darkness. Paul will later write to the Corinthians about "the light of the gospel of the glory of Christ" (2 Cor. 4:4), and affirm that "it is the God who commanded light to shine out of darkness who has shone in our hearts to give the light of the knowledge of the glory of God in the face of Jesus Christ" (4:6). From the time Paul saw the light on the Damascus road, his burning desire was to share that light with those who are still in darkness, as he had been.

Seeing the Risen Christ

All three accounts of Paul's conversion affirm that he heard a voice, but none of the three states expressly that he saw Jesus. Three days later in Damascus, however, Ananias, speaking prophetically, says, **"Brother Saul, the Lord Jesus, *who appeared to you* on the road as you came,..."** (Acts 9:17, italics added). We could presume that if Jesus had appeared, Paul would have seen Him, although it could also have been just the light and the voice. A clearer indication, however, comes when Paul goes to Jerusalem three years later and declares to the apostles how he had *seen the Lord* on the road (v. 27, italics added).

Further confirmations come from Paul as he later writes his letter to the Corinthians. There, he defends his apostolic authority with the rhetorical question, "Have I not seen Jesus Christ our Lord?" (1 Cor. 9:1). And he defends it again when speaking of Jesus' resurrection, "Then last of all He was seen by me also, as by one born out of due time" (15:8).

It is easy to assume that after Jesus appeared to Paul on the Damascus road, He has not made, nor does make, such visible appearances. Some theologians say as much when they discuss Paul's apostolic credentials. But, as a matter of fact, appearances of Jesus Himself, like the light of God's glory, are being reported with some regularity today, particularly in the two-thirds world.

It may be that we in the Western world are visited by Jesus less frequently or that our state of mind, including the state of mind in Christian circles, is such that we are not prepared to lend credibility to such reports and, therefore, those who may see Jesus would be reluctant to tell others.

But after seeing Jesus on the Damascus road, Paul subsequently had other similar experiences. For example, when he went back to the Temple in Jerusalem as a believer, Jesus appeared to him again. Paul says, **"Then it happened, when I returned to Jerusalem and was praying in the temple, that I was in a trance, and saw Him saying to me,..."** (Acts 22:17-18). Years later Luke records, **the following night the Lord stood by him [Paul] and said,...** (23:11). Paul probably saw Jesus many times.

Because Jesus is the same yesterday, today and forever, I believe we should not consider it particularly strange if we hear similar accounts today. *Christianity Today*, for example, published a story that seems to be authentic. In a certain province in China, where the gospel has been spreading like wildfire through many displays of power ministries reminiscent of the book of Acts, a woman who had never been in contact with Christians was suffering from an inoperable brain tumor. Jesus came to her, ministered to her and healed the brain tumor. Then He told her to travel to a certain nearby village where she would learn who He was. She obeyed, contacted a group of house church believers, learned that her "doctor's" name was Jesus Christ, and became a faithful Christian.[5]

Whether the risen Christ had been bodily present with this Chinese woman, as He had been with Thomas, or whether she had seen Him in a vision is not clear. At the end of the day, it really matters very little. A recent report from my friend Wolfgang Simson tells of Jesus using a dream to appear to a Muslim man in Egypt. This man had been Minister of Religious

Affairs under former President Sadat. He had sent his 12-year-old daughter to London for treatment for polio. While in the hospital, two Christian women prayed for her, she was instantly healed and she jumped out of bed.

Simson reports, "Just the night before, her Muslim father saw in a dream how Isa (Jesus) was standing next to the bed of his daughter. He saw Him putting His hand on her and healing her.

"The next day, he received a phone call from his daughter. Before she could tell her story, he said, 'Don't tell me what has happened because I already know. Jesus has healed you!'"[6]

Few Christian workers in Western nations have been called into ministry through visions or dreams, as was the apostle Paul. I was not called that way. Nonetheless, our call is no less authentic than if we had been. But elsewhere things are different.

Edward Murphy reports that a survey of West African Bible school students shows that dreams or visions were the most common way God had called them into ministry. The group surveyed was remarkable in that they represented an African church established by Western missionaries serving with a mission that was overtly noncharismatic and did not encourage power ministries. The missionaries there would not have been called through visions or dreams. Murphy says, "While this means of divine communication may not be as relevant in Western society, it is apparently very relevant in West African society...God accommodates Himself to human cultures as He seeks to communicate Himself to them."[7]

Falling to the Ground

26:14. And when we all had fallen to the ground,....

We know that all of those in Paul's traveling party saw the light. We also know that they heard a conversation going on, they did not see Jesus, nor were they able to pick up the words of the dialogue as Paul did. Acts 9 says: **the men who journeyed with him stood speechless, hearing a voice, but seeing no one (9:7)**, while Acts 22 adds: **"those who were with me...did not hear the voice of Him who spoke to me" (v. 9)**.

The phenomenon of people falling to the ground under the immediate manifestation of the power of God seems to be on the increase in Christian circles. Sometimes called "resting in the Spirit" or "slaying in the Spirit" or "falling under the power," it was common in the camp meetings and the brush arbor meetings of the early holiness movement of the last century,. and carried through the twentieth century by the Pentecostal and charismatic movements. In our day, it is being seen with growing frequency, including in some of the more traditional evangelical churches.

Two prominent figures identified with the traditional evangelical camp who have recently studied this phenomenon and written about it are Jack Deere and John White. Deere finds instances of falling in the power of the Spirit in the ministry of John Wesley and in the American Great Awakening, mentioned frequently by Jonathan Edwards.[8] John White tells of instances he has witnessed in Argentina and in the United States, in some cases many people falling at the same time, as they did on the Damascus road.

Although Deere and White both warn of carnal abuses and possible satanic counterfeits, they interpret this activity generally as a work of the Holy Spirit. John White describes a personal experience of being slain in the Spirit in these words: "I lay on my face, a quivering mass of adoring jelly. I, therefore, am unable to dismiss what I see of certain phenomena in the present, or what I read about in the past.[9]

Hearing the Voice of God

....

9:4. Then he fell to the ground, and heard a voice saying
to him, "Saul, Saul,...."
22:7. "And I fell to the ground and heard a voice saying
to me, 'Saul, Saul,....'"
26:14. ..."I heard a voice speaking to me and saying in the
Hebrew language, 'Saul, Saul,....'"

....

The voice Paul heard on the Damascus road was so clear he could
quote it verbatim; it was in his native language. Paul received a
revelation from God Himself. Later on, if someone had asked
Paul, "Why did you become a missionary to the Gentiles?" Paul
might well have answered, "Because God told me to."

Because power ministries are increasing so rapidly today, it is
becoming more common to hear Christian leaders justify decisions or actions by saying, "God told me to." The obvious potential of abusing this modus operandi is so great that many are ques-
tioning whether it has any place at all as a part of respectable
Christian behavior. Some refer to it as "extrabiblical revelation"
and argue that all of God's revelation is contained in the canon
of Scripture and that God does not engage in "present-day revelatory activity." This is why, according to this point of view, Paul
and others living before the canon was recognized needed to hear
directly from God more than we do today.

Recognizing that hearing from God can be, and at times is,
abused, we should nevertheless agree that it has substantial biblical precedence in both the Old Testament and the New
Testament. Pastor Jack Hayford has described it vividly: "As I say,
'God spoke to me,' I am being even more specific than referring
to general revelation or to private inner impressions. I reserve
these words intentionally for the rare, special occasions when, in

my spirit, I have had the Lord speak directly to me. I do not mean, 'I felt impressed' or 'I sensed somehow.' Instead, I mean that at a given moment, almost always when I least expected it, the Lord spoke *words* to me. Those words have been so distinct that I am virtually able to say, 'And I quote.'"[10]

Jack Hayford has gained such wide respect in Christian circles that few would see him as irresponsible or abusive in the use of the phrase "God told me to." At no time would Hayford, or any other responsible Christian, equate the words they hear from the Lord with Scripture. The incident in Acts 9 where Paul heard God's voice was later inscripturated by Luke, but this carries no implication that God has limited His direct communication to people or events recorded in the Bible. The Bible simply gives us examples of how God's nature is displayed through His actions.

How can we tell whether a person's affirmation that he or she has heard God's voice is correct or incorrect? It is good to keep in mind that the church functions as the Body of Christ and that each individual member is a part of the whole. When the Body of Christ is functioning well and when the fruit of the Spirit is normative as it should be, people who believe they have heard God's voice will seek confirmation from others before they make it public.

Churches and Christian groups would do well to use the following valuable three-stage filtering process in arriving at a consensus:

1. Was it a true word? Did the person hearing from God confuse a personal inner thought with the voice of God? Was more emotion than inspiration involved? Each one should be humble enough to admit that these are always possibilities.

2. Was the interpretation accurate? Even if the words were correctly heard, care needs to be taken in extracting the meaning, especially when the word is in poetic or parabolic form.

3. How is it to be applied? Should all, or any, of what God has

said be communicated to others? If so, to whom? What is God's timing for the application?

A consensus on such questions will help the Body of Christ receive the most benefit from divine communication.

Paul Continues to Damascus

....

9:6. So he, trembling and astonished, said, "Lord, what do You want me to do?" And the Lord said to him, "Arise and go into the city, and you will be told what you must do." 8. Then Saul arose from the ground, and when his eyes were opened he saw no one. But they led him by the hand and brought him into Damascus. 9. And he was three days without sight, and neither ate nor drank. 22:10. "So I said, 'What shall I do, Lord?' And the Lord said to me, 'Arise and go into Damascus, and there you will be told all things which are appointed for you to do.' 11. And since I could not see for the glory of that light, being led by the hand of those who were with me, I came into Damascus."

....

The tangle of thoughts and feelings running through Paul at this point in time must have been enormously confusing. Who knows if he didn't flash back to Stephen's death and his gracious words, "**Lord, do not charge them with this sin**" (7:60)? The Jesus whom Paul hated was now supernaturally drawing Paul into a loving, personal relationship. It would take Paul awhile to sort all of this out.

Simon Kistemaker says it as well as any: "What a reversal of events! Paul, who desired to dash the believers to the ground, is lying face down on the ground. He, who wished to bring prisoners bound from Damascus to Jerusalem, now is led as a prisoner of blindness into Damascus....He, who came to triumph over the Christian faith, now submits to the Captain of this faith."[11]

Paul's three-day blindness, which he attributes to the effects of the brilliant light he saw, would forever seal in his mind the stark contrast between light and darkness, a common theme in his later Epistles. His companions must not have seen the light so intensely, just as they did not hear the words as clearly, because they were not blinded. The significance of this blindness for Paul's conversion is pinpointed by Richard Rackham: "[Paul] is crucified with Christ, and the three days of darkness are like the three days in the tomb."[12] Paul would later write, "I have been crucified with Christ; it is not longer I who live, but Christ lives in me" (Gal. 2:20).

Paul's Commitment to the Body of Christ

Church growth leaders insist that the most complete understanding of what evangelism really is involves a twofold commitment: (1) commitment to Jesus Christ as Lord and Savior, and (2) commitment to the Body of Christ. Definitions of evangelism that see it as preaching only, or as registering decisions for Christ, are inadequate. Both preaching and decisions for Christ are essential, of course, but the process is not concluded until unbelievers become disciples of Jesus Christ and responsible members of His Church.

Paul's conversion was twofold. He committed himself to Jesus on the Damascus road, immediately referring to Jesus as "Lord." He committed himself to the Body of Christ in the city of Damascus, and the representative of the Church God had selected was Ananias.

Who was Ananias? Not the husband of Sapphira—the couple whose conspiracy of greed resulted in their death (see Acts 5:1-11)—but another man having the same name. He is one of the better-known figures in the New Testament, yet we know nothing about him other than his participation in Paul's conversion experience. He was significant in Paul's life, yet Paul never mentions him in his later Epistles. We know that he was a believer in Christ (see 9:10) and that he was a devout Jew, highly respected by fellow Jews (see 22:12).

We might be reminded that at that time most believers (the exceptions would be the Messianic Samaritans) were not regarded by themselves, or by the general public, as anything other than Jews or perhaps Messianic Jews. It is notable that God would choose, not an apostle nor a high-profile church leader, but what we would probably regard today as a layperson, to baptize and provide foundational spiritual instruction to the future Christian leader, second only to Jesus Christ.

9:10. Now there was a certain disciple at Damascus named Ananias; and to him the Lord said in a vision, "Ananias." And he said, "Here I am, Lord." 11. So the Lord said to him, "Arise and go to the street called Straight, and inquire at the house of Judas for one called Saul of Tarsus, for behold he is praying. 12. And in a vision he has seen a man named Ananias coming in and putting his hand on him, so that he might receive his sight." 13. Then Ananias answered, "Lord, I have heard from many about this man, how much harm he has done to Your saints in Jerusalem. 14. And here he has authority from the chief priests to bind all who call on Your name."
15. But the Lord said to him, "Go,...." 17. And Ananias went his way and entered the house; and laying his hands on him he said, "Brother Saul, the Lord Jesus, who appeared to you on the road as you came, has sent me that you may receive your sight and be filled with the Holy Spirit." 18. Immediately there fell from his eyes something like scales, and he received his sight

at once; and he arose and was baptized.
22:12. "Then one, Ananias, a devout man according to the
law, having a good testimony with all the Jews who dwelt
there, 13. came to me; and he stood and said to me,
'Brother Saul, receive your sight.' And at that same hour I
looked up at him. 14. Then he said,.... 16. 'And now why
are you waiting? Arise and be baptized, and wash away your
sins, calling on the name of the Lord.'"

Ananias's Remarkable Vision

We cannot say for sure, but it appears Ananias was unaware that
Saul the Terrible, as he must have been regarded by the disciples
who followed the Way, had actually arrived in Damascus.
However, Ananias did know Saul's reputation and that he was
bringing subpoenas from the high priests in Jerusalem. Here is the
second time in three days that Jesus actually appeared to a person
and spoke words so clearly that they could later be quoted.

The detail in this prophetic vision is remarkable. God told
Ananias specifically who the person was he should minister to
(Saul of Tarsus), exactly where he was (Judas's house on Straight
Street), what he was doing at the moment (praying), his new
condition (God's chosen vessel), and what Ananias was supposed
to do (lay on hands and heal the blindness). He also told
Ananias that Saul would be expecting him because Saul had
experienced a similar specific vision of **a man named Ananias
coming in and putting his hand on him** (9:12).

In the earlier years of my Christian experience, and later as an
ordained minister and missionary, I had no expectation whatsoever that God would desire to communicate important information to His people in this way. I did not doubt in the least that
He had done it to Ananias, but the Christianity I had been

taught, and was practicing, was heavy on knowledge and light on supernatural power. When I would hear of such things purportedly happening, I would usually relegate those who claimed to be experiencing them to the lunatic fringe and pay no more attention to them.

In recent years, however, as I have dedicated myself to researching the spiritual aspects of church growth and missiology, I have discovered that such specific prophecies are not at all uncommon today. My files contain documentation on many of them.

I recall a young man who came to one of my classes at Fuller Seminary some years ago. I asked him why he chose Fuller. He said he had been studying in another nationally known seminary, but he as a person, as well as his faith, seemed to be drying up. He began doubting whether he had really been called to the ministry and was considering leaving seminary and moving into another career. However, in prayer, he heard the voice of God telling him specifically to go to Fuller. The unusual thing about this was that at the time he knew nothing about Fuller. He didn't even know that a seminary by that name existed. The word was so specific, however, that he began inquiring and eventually learned that Fuller was indeed a seminary, far across the country on the West Coast. He obeyed the Lord, took the risk, came to Fuller and blossomed into a fruitful pastor and servant of God.

My friend could accurately have said, "I came to Fuller because God told me to." In a similar but more dramatic situation in the late 1980s, my friend John Wimber received a telephone call from Paul Cain, a man highly regarded for his gift of prophecy. He informed John that he was going to visit California soon because God had told him to. He said, furthermore, so that John would know it was truly God who was sending him, an earthquake would strike under Fuller Seminary the day he arrived. Paul Cain came, and on that day a powerful earthquake shook

Pasadena. Its epicenter was not exactly under Fuller Seminary, but rather it was under city hall, one block away. Close enough! I spent the next couple of days picking up books and putting them back on my shelves.

As I have said, accounts of such incidents could be multiplied. I mention them here to keep reminding us that I consider the book of Acts to be a training manual for modern Christians. Rather than some relic of the past, I see Acts as a contemporary guidebook for how the Christian faith most naturally spreads across cultures and around the world. Rather than reading Acts as a fascinating account of yesteryear, I like to read it with the expectation that God will continue to do the sort of things we see there, as His kingdom advances in our own day.

I have heard some say that although it might be possible that God speaks specifically to people today as He did in Acts, such a revelation should be limited to the individual person. They argue that it is excessively arrogant to expect God to say something through a person that might be directional for the whole Church. Paul's case, however, was much broader than him simply becoming a believer and receiving his sight after three days. It profoundly set the course for Christianity through the centuries. Let's look at this part of God's word to Paul.

Paul's Commission to the Nations

I mentioned awhile ago that Paul could have said he became a missionary because "God told me to." This word came to him not only directly from God (see Acts 22:15-18), but also through a prophecy given by a layperson, Ananias (see 9:15,16; 22:14,15).

....

9:15. "...he is a chosen vessel of Mine to bear My name before Gentiles, kings, and the children of Israel.

16. For I will show him how many things he
must suffer for My name's sake."
22:14. "...'The God of our fathers has chosen you that
you should know His will, and see the Just One, and hear
the voice of His mouth. 15. For you will be His witness to
all men of what you have seen and heard.'"
26:16. '...I have appeared to you for this purpose, to make
you a minister and a witness both of the things which you
have seen and of the things which I will reveal to you.
17. I will deliver you from the Jewish people, as well as
from the Gentiles, to whom I now send you, 18. to open
their eyes and to turn them from darkness to light, and
from the power of Satan to God, that they may receive
forgiveness of sins and an inheritance among those who
are sanctified by faith in Me.'

....

When he stood before King Agrippa years later, Paul called
this his "heavenly vision" (26:19) and could assure the king that
he had been obedient to it throughout his ministry.

It is unclear whether the words spoken by Jesus to Paul in Acts
22 were actually the direct words he heard on the road before
arriving in Damascus, or whether, as he was speaking to King
Agrippa, Paul simply telescoped them into a briefer summary. In
this passage, Paul does not mention either Ananias or his three
days of blindness. I see little value in laboring the point because
the effect is the same either way. Words from Jesus spoken
through legitimate personal prophetic utterances are no less valid
than those spoken by Jesus Himself to the person, whether by a
physical appearance, vision or dream.

It becomes highly important, however, that Paul's commission
was given to him by Jesus, whether through Ananias or other-

wise. Paul makes an issue of this when he later writes his letter to the Galatians. He introduces himself by saying, "Paul, an apostle (not from men nor through man, but through Jesus Christ and God the Father who raised Him from the dead)" (Gal. 1:1). Although Ananias spoke them, the words **he is a chosen vessel of Mine to bear My name before Gentiles, kings, and the children of Israel** (Acts 9:15) are commissioning words from Jesus to Paul. As F. F. Bruce says, Ananias was at this moment "[Christ's] mouthpiece," and "certainly a duly authorized prophet," and therefore, "it was Christ himself who commissioned Saul to be his ambassador."[13]

I myself can testify that receiving such commissioning words as these directly from Jesus brings powerful spiritual sustenance later on, especially when difficult times arise. Jesus told Paul **how many things he must suffer for My name's sake** (9:16). In 1989, at the massive Lausanne II Congress on World Evangelization in Manila, Philippines, God spoke to me in as clear, although less dramatic, a way as He spoke to Paul. He said, "I want you to take international leadership in the field of territorial spirits." At that time, issues surrounding territorial spirits, or what we now call "strategic-level spiritual warfare," were not common topics of conversation. The Congress itself, however, represented a breakthrough among its largely traditional evangelical constituency because no less than five workshops dealing with territorial spirits were offered there.

This was a kind of heavenly vision to me. Since then, I have become international coordinator of the Spiritual Warfare Network, I teach courses on that theme at Fuller Seminary and I have so far published three books on the subject. Much of what I have learned is reflected in parts of this commentary on Acts. But at the same time, I have been severely criticized and have suffered attacks of the enemy on myself and on my family.

At times, I read Paul's accounts of his own sufferings, his tribulations, imprisonments, stripes, times of sleeplessness, stonings, shipwrecks and many other difficulties in serving the Lord. Then I ask what has sustained him through all of those difficulties. Clearly, his heavenly vision. He was sure he was doing God's will because his commission had come directly from God. When I am down, personally, I also take heart because my commission, at least for this particular phase of my ministry, came directly from God. Seen in this light, I have no question in my mind about obeying the heavenly vision. I must do it.

The Apostle to the Uncircumcised

The Lord's commission to Paul combines the two major themes of the Acts of the Apostles: missiology and power ministries. Jesus said, **"I now send you, [to the Gentiles]...to turn them...from the power of Satan to God"** (26:17,18).

For those of us who are committed to world evangelization, this is the most important part of Paul's conversion experience. Paul was an unlikely candidate to be a missionary to the Gentiles. I am not exactly surprised that some of the commentators I am reading tend to take the opposite view and say that Paul's upbringing in Tarsus, a Gentile city, uniquely prepared him to minister to Gentiles.

One commentator, as I recall, speculates that Paul might have been an alumnus of the "University of Tarsus, reflecting the common knowledge that Tarsus, along with Alexandria and Athens, was a recognized center of what we today would call higher education." Anticipating this, I made a special point in the beginning of this chapter to explain that Paul was a *Hebrew* Jew as opposed to a *Hellenistic* Jew, that he was raised in a Jewish ghetto in Tarsus, and that at an early age his parents sent him to Jerusalem to be trained in rabbinic schools rather than in a Gentile-oriented educational system in Tarsus (see 22:3; 26:4). He undoubtedly spoke Greek, but in all probability had a Yiddish accent.

In the true sense of the word then, Paul was called to be an E-3 missionary. E-3 (i.e., evangelism three) is a technical term used in missiology to describe a radical cross-cultural gap. E-1 is monocultural evangelism and E-2 is cross-cultural, but the cultural gap from the missionary's home culture to that of the people to be evangelized is more moderate than for the E-3 missionary. God did not hesitate to recruit Paul for the most difficult of all missionary work. And the nature of some of the difficulties became clear when the apostles in Jerusalem, who were monoculturally oriented, had to come to terms with the nature of Paul's E-3 ministry in the Jerusalem Council more than 15 years later.

The Greek word for "Gentiles" translated here is *ethnos*, which also means nations—not nations in the geopolitical sense, but nations in the cultural sense. Our English word "ethnic" derives from *ethnos*. In modern missiology, we refer to these nations as "people groups." Jews are included among the world's people groups today, but when Paul was commissioned, *ethnos* meant specifically non-Jewish people groups. It is the same word Jesus used when He commissioned His disciples to "Go...and make disciples of all the *nations*" (Matt. 28:19, italics added).

Paul was also to witness to his own Jewish people. Jesus said he was **to bear My name before Gentiles [*ethne*], kings, and the children of Israel** (Acts 9:15). But Paul's primary calling was as an apostle to the Gentiles, the uncircumcision. In contrast, Peter's chief task was to be an apostle to the Jews, the circumcision. Paul later clearly writes about this when he says, "([God] who worked effectively in Peter for the apostleship to the circumcised also worked effectively in me toward the Gentiles)" (Gal. 2:8). As events continue to unfold, Peter did some work among Gentiles and Paul did some work among Jews, but essentially Paul was an E-3 missionary while Peter was an E-1 evangelist.

From the Power of Satan to God

Jesus not only commissioned Paul to evangelize the nations, but He also outlined his job description. He told Paul that when he entered a given people group he would find them under an awesome power, the power of Satan. His job would be **'to open their eyes and to turn them from darkness to light, and from the power of Satan to God'** (Acts 26:18).

This was no small task. Satan is none other than "the god of this age" (2 Cor. 4:4), and "the prince of the power of the air" (Eph. 2:2). The nations to which Paul was to take the message were all under the power of Satan and they had been for millennia. Satan fully intended to keep these nations under his dominion, and he was not willing to let any of them go without a fight. The fight would consist of what we call today "spiritual warfare." By the time Paul wrote Colossians and Ephesians nearly 30 years after he began his ministry, he had learned a great deal about spiritual warfare, saying, "We do not wrestle against flesh and blood, but against principalities, against powers, against the rulers of the darkness of this age, against spiritual hosts of wickedness in the heavenly places" (6:12).

Paul would also write, "For the weapons of our warfare are not carnal but mighty in God for pulling down strongholds" (2 Cor. 10:4). Biblical scholar Clinton Arnold examines all the weaponry mentioned in the writings of Paul and concludes, "If Paul were to summarize the primary way of gaining access to the power of God for waging successful spiritual warfare, he would unwaveringly affirm that it is through prayer."[14]

Paul had no option regarding whether or not he would engage in spiritual warfare as a part of his apostolic ministry to the nations. For the most part he did it well. Athens, as we shall see, was an exception. And Paul paid the price with the afflictions and tribulations he later describes, but he is clear on who ultimately wins. As he says to the Colossians, Jesus on the cross "disarmed principalities and powers, He made a pubic spectacle of them" (Col. 2:15).

As a result, many people, indeed, were taken from the power of Satan to God under the ministry of Paul, and multitudes have come from darkness to light through the spread of the gospel in subsequent centuries.

Paul in Damascus

Several other things happened to Paul in this memorable visit to Damascus.

> 9:17. And Ananias went his way and entered the house; and laying his hands on him he said, "Brother Saul, the Lord Jesus, who appeared to you on the road as you came, has sent me that you may receive your sight and be filled with the Holy Spirit." 18. Immediately there fell from his eyes something like scales, and he received his sight at once; and he arose and was baptized. 19. And when he had received food, he was strengthened....

Paul was not only healed spiritually, but he also experienced physical healing, ending three days of blindness. This came with the laying on of Ananias's hands. Laying on of hands is not a requirement for physical healing, but God often chooses to release His power through such a healing touch. Jesus said that as one of the signs that would follow His disciples "they will lay hands on the sick, and they will recover" (Mark 16:18).*

Paul was well prepared to receive Ananias's power ministry. He had been fasting for three days, and he was engaged in a time of prayer when Ananias arrived. Fasting, like the laying on of hands, is not a prerequisite for receiving the power of God, but fasting is a significant spiritual exercise that God honors.

In Paul's case, the healing was a bit more dramatic than it frequently is. As a physician, Luke would naturally be interested in recording what physiological changes might have taken place, and he tells us that something like scales fell from Paul's eyes. This brings to mind an occasion in Argentina when my friend Omar Cabrera prayed for a woman who had cataracts, and the physical cataracts literally fell from her eyes into her hands.

Without delay, Paul makes his profession of faith and commitment to the Body of Christ public through baptism. Although the details are not recorded here, we may safely assume that Ananias did the baptizing. We can also assume that Paul was filled with the Holy Spirit because Ananias said he had been sent to him **"that you may receive your sight and be filled with the**

---

*I am aware of the scholarly debate regarding the text at the end of the Gospel of Mark. As the center-column note in *The New King James Version* indicates, Mark 16:9-20 in the standard editions of the Greek New Testament are bracketed—suggesting they may not have been part of the Gospel when it was first written. Biblical scholars in the last few decades have been calling attention to the need to observe how the Bible was actually used in the churches. Kurt Aland, a leading textual scholar and organizing editor of both modern editions of the Greek testament, observes that Mark 16:9-20 "is found in 99 percent of the Greek manuscripts," and therefore over the centuries has by many Christians been regarded as Scripture. Technically inclined readers may read for themselves his comments (*The Text of the New Testament*, 2nd edition [Grand Rapids: William B. Eerdmans Publishing Co., 1989], 292F). If the longer ending were a later addition, it must mean that the Christians responsible felt it important to include these charismatic words of Jesus. Acts 20:35 shows that there were true words of Jesus that did not get recorded in the four Gospels (compare John 21:25).

Holy Spirit" (9:17). We have no further details, however, regarding how or when this happened or if any initial physical evidence was connected with the event.

The Life of a New Believer

....

9:19. ...Then Saul spent some days with the disciples at Damascus. 20. Immediately he preached the Christ in the synagogues, that He is the Son of God. 21. Then all who heard were amazed, and said, "Is this not he who destroyed those who called on this name in Jerusalem, and has come here for that purpose, so that he might bring them bound to the chief priests?" 22. But Saul increased all the more in strength, and confounded the Jews who dwelt in Damascus, proving that this Jesus is the Christ.

....

Paul spent time **with the disciples.** Imagine the joy of the believers when Saul the Terrible, instead of persecuting them, was baptized and decided to become one of them! Although Damascus was a Hellenized city, it also had a sizable resident Jewish community. It seems probable that before the Hellenistic Jewish believers had been ousted from Jerusalem following Stephen's death, some of the Damascus Jews had formed their own Messianic community and were worshiping Jesus. They still would have attended the synagogues because they continued to be Jews. Actually, the only ones who would have had reason to fear Saul's persecution would have been the recent arrivals from Jerusalem. Nevertheless, the whole Body of Christ probably prayed fervently for protection, and together they rejoiced when their prayers were answered to a degree much greater than they might have had faith to believe.

The reason the believers accepted their former enemy so readily was undoubtedly due to the bridges built by Ananias. Not only did they respect Ananias as a person, but the powerful and detailed prophecies he had received also built a great deal of confidence in the group that what was happening was clearly of God.

Paul also spent time **in the synagogues** (9:20) with the unbelieving Jews. Although the number is not known exactly, 40 or 50 Jewish synagogues could have been established in Damascus at that time. (In Jewish practice, only 10 adult males were needed to establish a synagogue.) Imagine the surprise of the Jews when the most notorious enemy of the Way came into their synagogues preaching that Jesus is indeed the way, the truth and the life! **All who heard were amazed** (9:21). They were caught off guard. Paul **was proving that this Jesus is the Christ** (9:22). The Greek word here denotes logical proofs, and Paul was probably applying some messianic passages from the Jewish Old Testament.

How is it that this new believer so rapidly **increased all the more in strength, and confounded the Jews** (9:22)? Certainly Paul was above average in intellect. As an opponent of Messianic Judaism, he had previously thought through the central issues, although now taking the opposite side. But much more than that, he later reveals that "the gospel which was preached by me is not according to man. For I neither received it from man, nor was I taught it, but it came through the revelation of Jesus Christ" (Gal. 1:11,12). Jesus Christ was Paul's mentor, and Paul had established such an intimacy with God that the kind of dialogue recorded on the Damascus road undoubtedly continued day after day. The fact alone that Paul was winning debates with Jewish rabbis shortly after his conversion, testifies to the extraordinary supernatural power accompanying his divine crash course.

A Spiritual Retreat in Arabia

How long did it actually take Paul to learn the theology he used to confound the rabbis? Luke does not make this clear for us. We read about **some days** in Acts 9:19 and **after many days were past** in 9:23. But later, when Paul tells his own story in the book of Galatians, he says that from the time of his conversion to the time Luke tells us he goes to Jerusalem in Acts 9:26, three years had passed (see Gal. 1:18). Some of these three years were spent in Damascus and some in Arabia. In Galatians Paul says, "I went to Arabia, and returned again to Damascus" (1:17).

The fact that Paul left Damascus to escape a plot to kill him indicates that he probably didn't go back right away. So the most likely sequence seems to be that fairly soon after his conversion he spent time in Arabia, a desert area east of Damascus, then went back for the ministry in the Damascus synagogues where the rabbis were amazed.

What was Paul doing in Arabia?

Because we have no specific details, the best we can do is speculate from other bits and pieces of information we do have. I would imagine that a good bit of his time in Arabia was spent working out the implications of the radical paradigm shift Paul had just experienced. Jesus, the Son of God, had now become the center of Paul's readjusted worldview. Because his center had changed, all of his thinking was up for revision.

As I have mentioned, Paul was receiving revelation directly from Jesus Christ, not from human teachers. Much of this has come down to us in the large section of the New Testament that Paul later wrote. Today, new converts also expect to hear from Jesus, but He speaks to us primarily through the written Word, which Paul did not have. Undoubtedly, Paul was working out the proofs that Jesus was the Messiah, proofs we read about in Acts 9:22.

Preaching to the Arabs?

Only a few of the commentaries I have seen surmise that Paul was also preaching to the Arabs. For example, F. F. Bruce says, "It certainly appears from a piece of evidence elsewhere in his correspondence that it was not simply a quiet retreat that Paul sought in Arabia."[15] Bruce does not mention this, but in Galatians 1 where Paul talks about his three years in Arabia and Damascus, he speaks of God's call to "preach Him [Christ] among the Gentiles" (Gal. 1:16).

More important, however, is what Paul later writes to the Corinthians: "In Damascus the governor, under Aretas the king, was guarding the city of the Damascenes with a garrison, desiring to apprehend me; but I was let down in a basket through a window in the wall, and escaped from his hands" (2 Cor. 11:32,33).

Aretas was the king of Arabia (more technically, the Nabataean kingdom). This extended almost up to the very walls of Damascus, and the Arab soldiers were waiting by the city gates to capture Paul if he should come out of the city.

But opposition occurred on a second front *within* the city:

··

9:23. Now after many days were past, the Jews plotted to kill him. **24.** But their plot became known to Saul. And they watched the gates day and night, to kill him. **25.** Then the disciples took him by night and let him down through the wall in a large basket.

··

It is obvious from what we have already seen why the Jews in Damascus were going after Paul. The rabbis were extremely unhappy with Paul's convincing arguments that Jesus was the true Messiah, as many rabbis also are today.

But why would the Arabs outside Damascus also be upset?

This is the evidence we have that points to the possibility Paul had spent some of his time in Arabia actively evangelizing. F. F. Bruce suggests, "The hostile interest which the Nabataean authorities took in him implies that he had done something to annoy them—something more than to withdraw to the desert for solitary contemplation."[16] He was also preaching the gospel.

So in all probability, during his time in Arabia, Paul was not only receiving his theology by revelation from Jesus Christ, but he was also beginning to apply what he was learning by witnessing to the Gentiles, as he had been commissioned to do on the Damascus road. We have no idea whether or not conversions occurred in Arabia, but we do know that, not surprisingly, Paul stirred up so much opposition, the government had to step in.

Apparently, then, this was the beginning of Paul's cross-cultural ministry. Instead of assuming that Paul's later ministry in Antioch was his first E-3 missionary experience, we have some reason to believe it could have begun in Arabia.

Back to Jerusalem

After his ignominious escape in a basket lowered at night over the city wall of Damascus, Paul decided to go back to Jerusalem.

> 26. And when Saul had come to Jerusalem, he tried to join the disciples; but they were all afraid of him, and did not believe that he was a disciple. 27. But Barnabas took him and brought him to the apostles. And he declared to them how he had seen the Lord on the road, and that He had spoken to him, and how he had preached boldly at Damascus in the name of Jesus. 28. So he was with them in Jerusalem, coming in and going out.

After three years, Paul was still between a rock and a hard place. The Jews considered him a traitor and an apostate—worse than Stephen—and some of them were trying to make him join

Stephen as a martyr. On the other hand, the believers in Jerusalem couldn't trust him. He had been the disciples' public enemy number one.

While Ananias builds the bridge to the disciples in Damascus, Barnabas, a respected pillar of the church in Jerusalem, builds the bridge here. Barnabas was living up to his name **Son of Encouragement**, which we read in Acts 4:36. Barnabas trusted Paul's credibility and took him to the apostles.

At first it might sound as though all 12 of the apostles would have been in Jerusalem, but this was not the case. Most of the apostles were by then out on the road, multiplying churches and training leadership for them. When Paul later writes about this visit, he says: "I went up to Jerusalem to see Peter, and remained with him fifteen days. But I saw none of the other apostles except James, the Lord's brother" (Gal. 1:18-19).

James was by then recognized as an apostle, but he was not one of the two named James belonging to the original 12. Among the original 12 were (1) James the son of Zebedee, also the brother of John, and (2) James the son of Alphaeus. The James whom Paul met was James the son of Joseph, Jesus' natural brother. This is the one who later wrote the book of James. He became Peter's successor as the leader of the Jerusalem church and played a prominent role in the Council of Jerusalem, which takes place about 15 years from this point, in A.D. 49.

When Paul wasn't talking with Peter and James, he was out preaching, especially to the Hellenists, the Greek-speaking Jews. They are the same ones who had Paul hold their coats while they were murdering Stephen, and then later tried to kill Paul also.

....

9:29. And he spoke boldly in the name of the Lord Jesus and disputed against the Hellenists, but they attempted to

kill him. 30. When the brethren found out, they brought
him down to Caesarea and sent him out to Tarsus.

The believers decided to send Paul away primarily because
they wanted to save his life, but it is probable they also thought
he was stirring up too much trouble. Like many new Christians,
Paul's enthusiasm may have been outweighing his wisdom at
the time.

But more important were Jesus' own words to Paul, which Paul
relates in Acts 22:

22:17. "Then it happened, when I returned to Jerusalem
and was praying in the temple, that I was in a trance
18. and saw Him saying to me, 'Make haste and get out
of Jerusalem quickly, for they will not receive your
testimony concerning Me.' 19. So I said, 'Lord, they know
that in every synagogue I imprisoned and beat those who
believe on You. 20. And when the blood of Your martyr
Stephen was shed, I also was standing by consenting to his
death, and guarding the clothes of those who were killing
him.' 21. Then He said to me, 'Depart, for I will send you
far from here to the Gentiles.'"

Paul recognized that the gospel was "for the Jew first" (Rom.
1:16), but he never did particularly well in evangelizing Jews. He
was called as an apostle to the uncircumcision, and this word of
Jesus in the Temple was a further confirmation of that call.

In missiological theory we talk of the harvest force and the
harvest field. A given field might be ripe enough, but if the
wrong harvester goes in, little fruit will be reaped. At this point
in time, unbelieving Hellenistic Jews were generally very receptive to the gospel, but Paul was not an anointed harvest force for

them. His anointing was to the Gentiles, so off he went to his hometown of Tarsus.

At this point, Paul drops out of the New Testament narrative for 10 years. It could be that he was ministering to the Gentiles in Syria and Cilicia, the area around Tarsus, but we do not know for sure. He comes back into the picture when his friend Barnabas invites him to join the missionary team, ministering to the new Gentile churches in Antioch in Acts 11.

The Churches Were Growing

Paul had stirred up so much trouble in Jerusalem, his departure made a big difference:

> 9:31. Then the churches throughout all Judea, Galilee, and Samaria had peace and were edified. And walking in the fear of the Lord and in the comfort of the Holy Spirit, they were multiplied.

Reflection Questions

1. Paul's dramatic conversion was not the only time a life has been radically changed by Jesus. Name some others you have known or heard about who had similar conversions.
2. Review and discuss the differences between Stephen's theology of mission and that of Paul (or Saul) before his conversion. This remains a central issue in our understanding of the book of Acts.
3. The possibility of God speaking directly to us one-on-one is rejected by some as "extrabiblical revelation." What are your thoughts on this phenomenon?
4. Try to describe in your own words what is meant by referring to Paul as an E-3 missionary. Why wasn't he an E-1 or E-2?

5. It seems that the Jerusalem church was better off not having Paul there than having him there on this early visit. Why would that be?

Notes

1. John Stott, *The Spirit, the Church and the World: The Message of Acts* (Downers Grove, IL: InterVarsity Press, 1990), pp. 168-169.
2. Richard N. Longenecker, *Paul: Apostle of Liberty* (New York: HarperCollins, 1964), p. 32.
3. F. F. Bruce, *Paul: Apostle of the Heart Set Free* (Grand Rapids: William B. Eerdmans Publishing Co., 1977), p. 43.
4. Jack W. Hayford, *Glory on Your House* (Grand Rapids: Chosen Books, 1991), pp. 63-67.
5. Sharon E. Mumper, "Where in the World Is the Church Growing?" *Christianity Today* (11 July 1986): 17.
6. Jim and Lyn Montgomery, "I myself will drive them out," *DAWN Ministries* newsletter (February 1994): 1.
7. Edward F. Murphy, "Church Growth Perspectives from the Book of Acts" (Ph.D. diss., Fuller Theological Seminary, 1979), 283.
8. Jack Deere, *Surprised by the Power of the Spirit* (Grand Rapids: Zondervan Publishing House, 1993), pp. 88-96.
9. John White, *When the Spirit Comes in Power* (Downers Grove, IL: InterVarsity Press, 1988), p. 24.
10. Hayford, *Glory on Your House*, p. 139.
11. Simon J. Kistemaker, *Exposition of the Acts of the Apostles* (Grand Rapids: Baker Book House, 1990), p. 335.
12. Richard Belward Rackham, *The Acts of the Apostles* (London: Methuen & Co., Ltd., 1901), p. 133.
13. F. F. Bruce, *The Book of Acts* (Grand Rapids: William B. Eerdmans Publishing Co., 1954; revised edition, 1988), p. 188.
14. Clinton E. Arnold, *Powers of Darkness* (Downers Grove, IL: InterVarsity Press, 1992), p. 158.
15. Bruce, *Paul: Apostle of the Heart Set Free*, p. 81.
16. Bruce, *The Book of Acts*, p. 192.

CHAPTER

2

Acts 9, 10 & 11

Peter Blazes the Trail to the Gentiles

The message of the Way was spreading rapidly through Jerusalem, Judea, Samaria and nearby lands. Awhile back, Luke had reported, **the word of God spread, and the number of disciples multiplied greatly** (Acts 6:7). Now, as we have just seen, **the** *churches* **throughout all Judea, Galilee, and Samaria...were multiplied** (9:31, italics added). From the multiplication of *disciples* we now move to the multiplication of *churches*. This is a geometrical increase.

The Most Effective Evangelism

Nothing is more important in developing a strategy for evangelizing a given geographical area than multiplying new churches. I continue to affirm what I have said and written on many occasions: "The single most effective evangelistic methodology under heaven is planting new churches."[1] This axiom not only applies to areas where Christian churches have not previously existed, but it also applies to areas where Christianity may have been present for centuries.

In the same way the gospel spreads throughout the book of Acts, it also spreads through multiplying churches. No other way is possible. The definition of what a church is, or what it may not be, will vary. In my opinion, wherever a group of believers meets together on a regular basis to celebrate their mutual faith in Jesus Christ as Savior and Lord, where they lift their voices together in worship and praise to God Almighty, where they are committed to each other in ministry and loving care, and where they agree to obey God to the best of their abilities, there we find a church. It can take many forms—from a group meeting under a tree in Indonesia, to a weekly meeting of Christian university students in a dorm, to believers congregating in a hotel conference room in Argentina, to worshipers gathering in a cathedral in England, to disciples huddled in a house in China with its doors closed.

Evangelism is most effective when it demands the kind of dual commitment we saw Paul make in chapter 1: a commitment to Jesus Christ as Lord and a commitment to the Body of Christ. When seen in this light, evangelism intrinsically requires multiplying churches.

Sometimes the church planting is monocultural. In practice, the vast majority of church plants anywhere are monocultural. From the viewpoint of worldwide evangelistic strategy, however, the most significant church planting is done by those called of God to break cross-cultural boundaries and to establish the first vital outposts of Christianity in a previously unreached people group. When this is done well, monocultural (E-1) church planting then takes over for the long haul, but it cannot begin without initial cross-cultural (E-2 and E-3) church planting.

Why Peter?

Peter was the person called by God to blaze the trail for church planting among the Gentiles. I say "blaze the trail" because that's about all he did. Peter has gone down in history as an apostle to the circumcision, to his own people group—the Jews. Paul is the one who later becomes the most prominent church planter among Gentiles. But God had specific and significant reasons for selecting Peter to minister in the house of Cornelius and to baptize him and his family. Peter might be seen as Paul's equivalent of Jesus' John the Baptist.

The most important consideration was that Peter at this time was regarded as the leader of the establishment apostles. Along with James and John, he was seen as a "pillar of the church" (see Gal. 2:9). When the issue of Gentile conversion comes to a head later in Acts 15, it is Peter's theology, forged in the house of Cornelius, that sets the tone for the final decision. Because, as I have previously said, theology in general tends to emerge from ministry (and usually not vice versa), an essential part of God's plan for subsequent world evangelization was to compel Peter to engage in a relatively brief time of cross-cultural ministry.

I say "compel" because Peter likely would not have chosen to evangelize Gentiles on his own. God, as we will see, resorted to some extraordinary manifestations of supernatural power in this case to convince Peter to go into Cornelius's house. Peter simply did not have the missionary gift. What is the missionary gift? In my book *Your Spiritual Gifts Can Help Your Church Grow*, I define the missionary gift as follows: "The gift of missionary is the special ability that God gives to some members of the Body of Christ to minister whatever other spiritual gifts they have in a second culture."[2] To say that Peter did not have the missionary gift is not to consider him a second-class citizen—my best estimate is that something like only one percent of all Christians have the gift.

It is regrettable that some confuse the missionary gift with the gift of apostle. At least one version of the Bible inadvisably translates the Greek *apostolos* (apostle) as "missionary." Peter was an example of one who had the gift of apostle but not the gift of missionary. Paul, on the other hand, had both the gift of apostle and the gift of missionary. This will become evident when later we look at some friction between the two, which Paul writes about in Galatians.

Although he did not have a missionary gift, Peter was God's icebreaker not only with the Gentiles in Cornelius's house, but also as we have seen, with the Samaritans, moving into Samaria as Philip was leading a great movement toward God. Before we get to Peter's ministry to the Gentiles, we will first look at some of his more usual monocultural ministry in Judea.

The Harvest in Lydda and Sharon
Acts 9

32. Now it came to pass, as Peter went through all parts of the country, that he also came down to the saints who dwelt at Lydda. 33. There he found a certain man named Aeneas, who had been bedridden eight years and was paralyzed. 34. And Peter said to him, "Aeneas, Jesus the Christ heals you. Arise and make your bed." Then he arose immediately. 35. So all who dwelt at Lydda and Sharon saw him and turned to the Lord.

Peter spent some of his time in itinerant ministry, planting churches, encouraging believers and training leaders. It says here that he **went through all parts of the country.** In all probability, each of the 12 apostles was doing similar things. We recall that when Paul arrived in Jerusalem from Damascus, only one of them, Peter, happened to be there.

A church had already been planted in the city of Lydda, located in the plain of Sharon in western Judea. How the church was started we do not know for sure, but in all possibility Philip could have evangelized in Lydda after he baptized the Ethiopian eunuch and was caught away by the Holy Spirit. We are told that Philip then preached in all the cities till he came to Caesarea (8:40). Lydda happened to be in that region.

Paralyzed Eight Years and Healed

I would imagine that many dramatic things took place in Lydda through the ministry of the Holy Spirit, but undoubtedly the most notable was the miraculous healing of Aeneas who had been paralyzed for eight years. Aeneas might have been a believer, but more likely he was an unbeliever—as was the lame man at the gate of the Temple who was also healed by Peter when Peter was accompanied by John.

The technical line between a healing and a miracle may be impossible to draw because of the wide area of overlap. However, there seems to be some distinction because in the list of spiritual gifts in 1 Corinthians 12, both "gifts of healings" (v. 9) and "the working of miracles" (v. 10) appear as separate items. If it is legitimate to say so, it would seem to me that a man who had been paralyzed for eight years and instantly started to walk would fall more into the miracle category. In the healing ministry I personally have done over the past few years, I have seen literally hundreds of people healed from chronic back pain, but I have yet to see a paralyzed person who has come to me in a wheelchair get out of the wheelchair and walk. I know that God does this through others today just as He did in Lydda, but as yet not through me. That is why I am willing to affirm that I have the spiritual gift of healing, but not the gift of miracles.

One of the most remarkable things about the healing of Aeneas was that Peter did not pray for him, as far as we are told. He simply made a declaration: **"Aeneas, Jesus the Christ heals you. Arise and make your bed"** (9:34).

Healing stories in the New Testament often seem a good bit simpler than the healing ministries in some of our churches today. Whether the power of God was more immediate and easier to get in touch with in those days I do not know. True, when we conscientiously develop divine healing ministries over some years, it is not unusual from time to time to see miraculous healings equal to, or possibly surpassing, the drama accompanying the events we read about in the Gospels and Acts. But they are clearly the exceptions, not the rule. Could it be that the pattern of Matthew, Mark, Luke and John was to single out such exceptions and write about them? We know that John carefully selected seven outstanding miracles around which to structure his whole Gospel. If this were the biblical pattern, it would be a considerable consolation to those of us who struggle from day to day and week to week with what seems at times to be unduly limited access to the power of God.

Because of this, the people I know who have a healing ministry rarely make the kind of declaration Peter made in Lydda. I teach my students at Fuller to take a more cautious approach and to be a bit more tentative in their conclusions about what might have happened. The exception to this comes on the rare occasions when we get a strong word from the Lord during the prayer time, that in this particular case the healing will be instant and complete. Something like this must have happened to Peter. [Aeneas] arose immediately (9:34).

A "Lyddic" People Movement

The evangelistic results of the healing were awesome. **All who** dwelt at Lydda and Sharon saw him and turned to the Lord (9:35). Although this may be a case where the biblical "all" should be taken figuratively instead of literally, a large segment of the population of the city and the surrounding plain of Sharon became disciples of Jesus. The description is that of a classic people movement, so much so that missiologist Donald McGavran, one of the chief theoreticians of the field, labels one of his five types of people movements "Lyddic movements." In a Lyddic movement, McGavran says, "The entire community becomes Christian."[3]

Such a thing actually happens on occasion, and one of our hopes is that the frequency will increase considerably as we move forward in world evangelization. In some nations, entire Muslim villages have declared themselves Christian overnight. In the Beoga Valley of Irian Jaya, the entire Uhunduni people group of 4,500 made a joint decision to become Christian and publicly burned their fetishes. A large commune in mainland China declared itself Christian and the commune became known as "Jesus Mountain." Whole Aymara townships in the Bolivian Andes have decided to turn to the gospel from one day to the next. Reports have recently begun to filter out of the Himalaya Mountains, telling of former "lama villages" that are now "Jesus villages."

Honoring Group Decisions

A people movement, McGavran says, is "a multi-individual, mutually-interdependent conversion."[4] This is important in missiology, because in most non-Western parts of the world all important decisions are group, as opposed to individual, decisions. This may sound strange to us Westerners who have been taught to hold rugged individualism as a high cultural value. But our way of expecting each person to step out from the group and make a personal decision to follow Jesus Christ makes no sense to many peoples of our world today. To many peoples, it appears that if it is up to each person, then accepting Christ must not be an important decision because in their minds all of life's *important* decisions are made by the group, never by individual people violating their commitment to each other and stepping out on their own.

It would be reasonable to expect that something like this would have happened in Lydda. It is doubtful that Peter would have preached a sermon, invited inquirers to come forward, and had a team of counselors to interview each person and pray with each one to receive Jesus as Savior and Lord. Rather, the leaders and opinion makers of Lydda would have reflected on the public testimony of the small group of disciples that was already in their city, examined the evidence presented by Peter in both word and deed, and over a period of time come to a community consensus that Jesus was truly the Messiah they had been waiting for through the centuries.

As is characteristic of people movements, this decision would not have involved crossing racial, linguistic or cultural barriers. They were not asked to join up with Gentiles or Samaritans. Their established relationships with their families, their friends and their synagogues would have remained intact. It was a religious or spiritual decision they were willing to make on its own merits, and they did. **All...Lydda and Sharon saw him and turned to the Lord** (9:35).

The thing that triggered the people movement in Lydda was that they **saw him,** referring to Aeneas who had been paralyzed for eight years and was now walking. This public display of the power of God was the "deed" part of Peter's ministry. Luke seems to highlight this in Acts. He speaks of Jesus attested by **"miracles, wonders, and signs"** (Acts 2:22), of the apostles in

Jerusalem doing **many wonders and signs** (2:43), of Stephen doing **great wonders and signs among the people** (6:8), of **the miracles which he** [Philip] **did** (8:6), and of **signs and wonders to be done by their** [Paul and Barnabas's] **hands** (14:3). In fact, in people movements today such a form of power ministry is often (although not always) the catalyst that serves as the principal "sign" to point people to the Savior.

A vivid illustration comes out of mainland China where a 70-year-old woman was the leader of a secret house church, the only one who knew where the Bibles were hidden or who could be trusted. When she suddenly died of a heart attack, her family was shocked and prayed to God that she would come back to life. Carl Lawrence tells it this way: "After being dead two days, she came back to life. She scolded her family for calling her back. They reasoned with her. They said they would pray that in two days she could return to the Lord. It would take that much time to set the matters straight."[5] Sure enough, after two days she told her family she was seeing angels coming to her and she went to be with the Lord.

The result? The entire Chinese village, like Lydda, turned to the Lord.

Raising the Dead

Such a story, as this one out of China, raises questions in many minds. It may seem too farfetched to some. Does God *really* raise people from the dead? While he was still in Lydda, a call came to Peter that will allow us to examine this matter of the dead being raised in some detail.

....

9:36. At Joppa there was a certain disciple named Tabitha, which is translated Dorcas. This woman was full of good works and charitable deeds which she did. 37. But it hap-

pened in those days that she became sick and died. When
they had washed her, they laid her in an upper room. 38.
And since Lydda was near Joppa, and the disciples heard
that Peter was there, they sent two men to him, imploring
him not to delay in coming to them.

Peter received an urgent, unexpected call from Joppa, brought
by two brothers from the church there. This was another church,
in all probability, first planted by Philip (see 8:40). Joppa, a harbor on the Mediterranean Sea, was about a three-hour trip from
Lydda. One of the highly respected women of the church,
Dorcas, had suddenly died. She was respected because of her
many good deeds done through her obvious spiritual gifts of
mercy and service.

Word had come to the believers in Joppa that Peter was in nearby Lydda. They probably had received word of the healings and
miracles going on there, Aeneas being one of the outstanding
examples. Peter's gift of healing would have by then been well
known among the Messianic Jews in Joppa. It may have been that
some of them, or their relatives, would have been among those
who took the sick to Jerusalem where the power of God was so
strong that even Peter's shadow was healing the sick (see 5:15,16).

Although we have no reason to affirm that raising the dead
had been taking place as an ongoing part of the ministry of the
apostles and others in those days, we have no reason to deny it
either. It would seem somewhat likely, considering that the first
time Jesus sent out Peter and the other disciples to preach the
message of the kingdom of God, He commanded them to "Heal
the sick, cleanse the lepers, *raise the dead*, cast out demons"
(Matt. 10:8, italics added). If that were the case, then calling on
Peter to minister to Dorcas might not appear to be a totally
unreasonable request on the part of the church at Joppa.

Dorcas was really dead. Her expiration had been reported by Luke, a recognized physician. I point this out because as I have researched the phenomena connected with signs and wonders in the world today, I have found that some, who prefer not to believe that miracles of the magnitude of raising the dead could be occurring, argue their point by casting doubt on whether the subject was really dead at all. Muslims do this, for example. They refuse to believe that Jesus was raised from the dead, so they explain the obvious historical facts away by denying that He actually died on the cross.

One American professor refused to believe that the dead were being raised, as reported in the great Indonesia revival of 1965-1970, because after field research he concluded that the Indonesian concept of death was different from ours. I find this somewhat ludicrous, however, because Indonesians, like Americans, bury only dead people. In fact, day by day the average Indonesian has much more direct contact with death than the average American.

"Tabitha, Arise"

9:39. Then Peter arose and went with them. When he had come, they brought him to the upper room.... 40. But Peter put them all out, and knelt down and prayed. And turning to the body he said, "Tabitha, arise." And she opened her eyes, and when she saw Peter she sat up.
41. Then he gave her his hand and lifted her up; and when he had called the saints and widows, he presented her alive.

Just to call Peter to walk for three hours to minister to Dorcas was in itself evidence that the believers in Joppa had an extraordinarily high level of faith. It would be reasonable to expect that much prayer and intercession had been in progress there. They probably had high expectations that Dorcas would be healed. Unlike some dramatic instances of power ministries, such as the healing of the lame man at the Temple gate (see Acts 3), this one was fully premeditated.

They brought him to the upper room....But Peter put them all out. Why? From what has just been said, I do not think it was because of their unbelief. Peter could have been trying to avoid embarrassment in case nothing happened, but I doubt that as well. A more likely possibility is that he was following the pattern he himself had observed when Jesus raised Jairus's daughter from the dead. On that occasion, Jesus permitted no one to follow Him except Peter, James and John and the parents of the girl (see Mark 5:37,40).

Although techniques should not be seen as a determining factor in divine healing or miracles, it is a fact that many who engage in power ministries tend to mirror the behavior of their mentors. If their mentors' hands tremble while praying for the sick, the disciples' hands may tremble also. Using oil, singing certain worship songs, praying in a distinct tone of voice, reciting liturgical prayers and many other behavioral patterns seem to be transmitted through a kind of spiritual genetics. Peter gives us an example by sending the mourners out of the room, as his mentor, Jesus, had done.

We are not told if Peter prayed when he healed Aeneas. But in this case, when the others had left, **Peter...knelt down and prayed** (Acts 9:40). What did he pray? I would think Peter would have been asking God to make clear to him what His will was in this particular case. The more difficult a power ministry assignment, the more necessary it is to be as sure as is possible of God's will. Raising the dead is obviously near the apex of difficulty, at least from a human perspective. On a few occasions, I have approached the Lord to seek His will about praying that the dead would be raised, but I have received a negative response each time. By the time he finished praying, Peter, and those with him, knew that this was God's will and God's time.

This is why Peter could take the direct approach, as he had done with Aeneas. He used a direct command: **"Tabitha [Dorcas], arise."** God apparently had already restored life to the dead body while Peter was praying. How much of Peter's prayer had also included petition we do not know. But he might have said something like, "Father, I bring this dear saint of God before you and ask that you honor the prayers of the church and restore life to her." In any case, before he finished praying, Peter knew God had said yes.

Dorcas sat up, and the church rejoiced to see her alive!

Evangelistic Results

Although healings and miracles have intrinsic value, such as relieving pain or allowing lame people to walk or blessing the congregation at Joppa with the renewed presence of Dorcas whom they loved so much, more importantly, they are "signs." They are signs of the kingdom of God. They are signs that point to Jesus Christ as the Lord of lords. God desires to use these signs to bring unbelievers to salvation.

God used this miracle in Joppa for that purpose:

> **42. And it became known throughout all Joppa, and many believed on the Lord.**

The faith of the believers in Joppa at that moment must have been about as high as it can possibly go. Everyone in the city soon heard about Dorcas, and great power occurred in witnessing.

However, it is notable that although **all who dwelt at Lydda and Sharon...turned to the Lord** (9:35), in Joppa all heard about it, but Luke says, **many believed on the Lord** (v. 42). The results were good, but not as good as they were in Lydda. Why?

The first part of the answer to this puzzle is that many factors influence the growth and nongrowth of churches besides the effects of miracles and power encounters. Any number of differences, of which we are totally unaware, could have explained why a virtual "clean sweep" occurred in Lydda, but something short of that occurred in Joppa. Actually, the magnitude of the miracle was greater in Joppa, but not the total evangelistic outcome.

If the hypotheses we are developing concerning strategic-level spiritual warfare have some validity, they could provide a possible explanation. Although Luke doesn't furnish the specific details for us, it might have been that related to the healing of Aeneas in Lydda, the territorial spirits or strongmen over the city were bound and they, therefore, loosed their grip on the unsaved people there. For some reason, a similar thing might not have happened in Joppa when Dorcas was raised from the dead. It could have been that the principality over Lydda was attached to Aeneas himself, just as the principality over western Cyprus was apparently dominating the sorcerer Bar-Jesus or Elymas, according to the interpretation I will later suggest in Acts 13.

What Do We Learn from Seeing the Dead Raised?

Here we have the first, but not the last, case of a dead person being raised in the book of Acts. Another case will come when Paul ministers in Lystra (see Acts 14). In the biblical narrative, we now switch from Jesus the Son of God raising dead people, such as Jairus's daughter and Lazarus and then being raised from the dead Himself, to a human being, Peter, serving as God's instrument to do it. What do we learn from this?

Raising the dead is a Christian ministry. It obviously is not part of the normal ministry of an average church, but it is something that pleases God to do through His people from time to time. As I have mentioned, it was part of the commission Jesus gave His disciples when He first sent them out on their own. Among other things, He told the 12 to "raise the dead" (Matt. 10:8).

Raising the dead represents only a partial victory over death. For one thing, all those who were raised from the dead, with the exception of Jesus Himself, eventually died again. Secondly, death remains a tragic human phenomenon. No one lives forever physically.

The ultimate cause of death is Satan. Satan made it happen first in the Garden of Eden, and since then, all human beings must pay the price for the imputed sin of Adam and Eve. "The wages of sin is death" (Rom. 6:23). We all must die unless we are fortunate enough to be on earth during the rapture: "We who are alive and remain shall be caught up together with them in the clouds to meet the Lord in the air" (1 Thess. 4:17).

Death is not God's original intention for humans, nor is death a feature of the full kingdom of God. Death will one day be cast into the lake of fire (see Rev. 20:14). Paul calls death the "last enemy" (1 Cor. 15:26). In the New Jerusalem, "God will wipe away every tear from their eyes; there shall be no more death" (Rev. 21:4).

In light of this, raising the dead is a sign of the kingdom of God. When Jesus once listed the signs of the kingdom to reassure John the Baptist that He was the true Messiah, He included the fact that "the dead are raised" (Luke 7:22). This, among many other things, proves that the kingdom of God is among us, although not yet in its fullness. Every dead person raised is a direct insult to Satan. It is a foretaste of the final victory over the "last enemy." Death may still be with us, but it is on the way out. Meanwhile, the effects of physical death are nullified by eternal life for those who believe in Jesus Christ.

The underlying purpose of raising the dead, I repeat, is to display a sign of the power of God so that people will be saved: **And it became known throughout all Joppa, and many believed on the Lord** (Acts 9:42).

The Breakthrough to the Gentiles
Acts 10

The account of Peter going to the house of the Gentile Cornelius is the longest story told by Luke in the book of Acts. The three stories that take up the most space are:

- Peter and Cornelius (Acts 10—11)—77 verses
- Stephen's speech and death (Acts 6—7)—67 verses
- Paul's conversion (Acts 9, 22 and 26)—61 verses

What do all three stories have in common? They are all crucial incidents related to breaking the cultural barriers in order for the gospel to move from Jews to non-Jews. This is another indication that Acts should be read and understood as essentially a missiological document if we are to receive its maximum value for our lives and our ministries. Let's once again refresh our memories about Luke's central theme in the book of Acts:

> **1:8. But you shall receive power when the Holy Spirit has come upon you; and you shall be witnesses to Me in Jerusalem, and in all Judea and Samaria, and to the end of the earth.**

God Speaks to Cornelius

The story begins with God speaking a word directly to Cornelius:

....

10:1. There was a certain man in Caesarea called
Cornelius, a centurion of what was called the Italian
Regiment, 2. a devout man and one who feared God with
all his household, who gave alms generously to the people,
and prayed to God always.

....

Caesarea was a Gentile city, 30 miles north of Joppa, where
Peter had been ministering after raising Dorcas from the dead.
Although Caesarea was predominantly Gentile, many Jews also
resided there, and several synagogues were located there.

As a centurion, Cornelius would have been a captain of the
Roman army in charge of 100 soldiers. Each Roman legion comprised 3,000 to 6,000 men and was divided into 10 cohorts (300-
600 each) and 60 centuries (100 each when at full strength).

It is significant that Cornelius was **one who feared God with
all his household.** At that time, by far the most receptive
Gentiles to the gospel of Christ were these "God-fearers" such
as Cornelius. As I mentioned at the close of the first volume on
Acts, the Ethiopian eunuch who was led to Christ by Philip in
the Gaza Strip was not only the first Gentile convert of whom
we have record, but was also in all probability another God-
fearer.

Who Were the "God-Fearers"?

First-century Jews, unlike Jews today, were aggressively evangelistic. It was customary for Jews to send out proselytizing bands
into Gentile regions to seek converts called "proselytes." Recall
that the Jewish theology of the day taught that the only way a
human being could be reconciled to Jehovah God was by first
becoming a Jew. Outside of Judaism, salvation was not possible.

The evangelistic message was, "Find God—be a Jew!" And

this message received considerable response. Society in many parts of the Roman Empire had become so corrupt, and life for many was so hopeless, that many of them were looking for serious answers to their questions about the meaning of life. Some were strongly attracted to the monotheism and high moral and ethical standards of the Jewish faith. They were impressed by the lifestyle of the Jewish community and desired to become a part of it and to worship Jehovah.

For people to become a part of the Jewish faith, the process involved a threefold rite, according to F. F. Bruce:

1. "Circumcision (for male proselytes),
2. "A purificatory self-baptism in the presence of witnesses, and
3. "The offering of a sacrifice (while the Jerusalem temple stood)."[6]

These obviously were demanding requirements, but many were willing to accept them, and Jewish proselytes were to be found in many of the synagogues throughout the Roman Empire. It is important to understand that once Gentiles became proselytes, they were no longer Gentiles. They, their families and the Jews themselves considered them from that day on to be Jews and not Gentiles.

Understandably, many Gentiles would be attracted to the monotheism and the high ethical standards of the Jews, but were not prepared to take the radical step of becoming proselytes and making a total break with their Gentile roots. Recognizing this, the Jews of the day had created a special place for them in their synagogue communities as "God-fearers." They had a recognized affiliation with the synagogue, they worshiped the God of the Jews, and they agreed to adhere to the Jewish law to the best of their abilities, observing the Sabbath and the dietary laws as strictly as they thought they could.

When they went to synagogue meetings, however, the God-fearers had to congregate in a separate designated place. They could not enter the worship area of the synagogue itself because they were still *Gentiles*, and as such were regarded by Jews as unclean. We need to understand this thoroughly to give us a backdrop for comprehending the magnitude of Peter's ministry to Cornelius, one of these God-fearers. John Stott says, "It is difficult for us to grasp the impassable gulf which yawned in those days between the Jews on the one hand and the Gentiles (including even the 'God-fearers') on the other....No orthodox Jew would ever enter the home of a Gentile, even a God-fearer, or invite such into his home."[7]

For reasons that will become clearer as we move on, the God-fearers, more than any other category of Gentiles, were open to hearing the gospel and receiving Jesus as their Messiah. It could well be that the absence of any evangelistic fruit from Paul's ministry in Arabia (see chapter 1), at least any worthy of mention by Luke, may have been due to the absence of God-fearers. Paul may have learned by trial and error that ordinary Gentiles (such as Arabs) at that time were not a particularly ripened harvest field, but he later discovered decisively that the God-fearing Gentiles were definitely ripe.

God Had Prepared Cornelius

Two special qualities seem to make Cornelius stand out from the average God-fearer. First, Cornelius **gave alms generously to the people** (10:2). He was practicing what Jesus called the second commandment, in loving his neighbor as himself. This did not save him, but it helped prepare him for conversion.

Second, Cornelius **prayed to God always** (10:2). Cornelius had come into a relationship with God to the extent that God knew his name, as we shall see. God chose to contact Cornelius in the "ninth hour," or 3:00 P.M., which was a normal Jewish hour of prayer.

An Angel Visits Caesarea

3. About the ninth hour of the day he saw clearly in a vision an angel of God coming in and saying to him, "Cornelius!" 4. And when he observed him, he was afraid, and said, "What is it, lord?" So he said to him, "Your prayers and your alms have come up for a memorial before God."

When Cornelius tells the story later, he adds:

30. "Four days ago I was fasting until this hour; and at the ninth hour I prayed in my house, and behold, a man stood before me in bright clothing, 31. and said, 'Cornelius, your prayer has been heard, and your alms are remembered in the sight of God.'"

As Luke records it, the angel came in a vision, and when Cornelius tells it later, he does not mention a vision but he speaks of the angel himself. Angels do appear in bodily form and they also appear in visions. The important thing for Cornelius was that somehow he saw a man in the room dressed in bright clothing and recognized that man to be an angel. If the angel came as an answer to prayer, what could Cornelius's prayer have been? Not only had he been praying that day, but he had been fasting as well. Knowing that what was about to happen came as a direct answer to Cornelius's prayer, his prayer must have been a cry of his heart to know God personally. His affiliation with the synagogue would have allowed him to recognize God theologically as the Creator of heaven and earth, but he now desired a personal relationship so that God would truly become his Father. In a word, he wanted to be saved.

The angel's instructions were simple:

> 5. "Now send men to Joppa, and send for Simon whose surname is Peter. 6. He is lodging with Simon, a tanner, whose house is by the sea. He will tell you what you must do."

We later learn more of what the angel meant:

> 11:14. '[Peter] will tell you words by which you and all your household will be saved.'

I find the detail of this remarkable. This story leaves little room to doubt that it is part of the very nature of God to communicate specifically to human beings. The angel knew Cornelius's name, Peter's two names, Peter's address and, of course, the content of Cornelius's petition. Such words from God bring forth an immediate desire to obey, which Cornelius did:

> 10:7. And when the angel who spoke to him had departed, Cornelius called two of his household servants and a devout soldier from among those who waited on him continually. 8. So when he had explained all these things to them, he sent them to Joppa.

Reflecting back to chapter 1, Cornelius could have honestly said he sent the three to Joppa "because God told me to."

Peter's Famous Vision: Animals in a Sheet

10:9. The next day, as they went on their journey and drew
near the city, Peter went up on the housetop to pray, about
the sixth hour. 10. Then he became very hungry and wanted
to eat; but while they made ready, he fell into a trance.

As with Cornelius, God chose to communicate directly to Peter
while he was setting aside a specific, probably routine, time to
pray. This time it was not through an angel, but by the Holy
Spirit (see 10:19). Sometimes we resist establishing and following a rigid, predetermined daily schedule for prayer. We say we
want to avoid "legalism" or we don't want to "get into a rut." I
believe it is significant that at this hinge point in history God
chose to honor the routine, established prayer times of both
Cornelius and Peter, speaking to them clear and directive words
precisely then. Something about such seemingly routine habits of
prayer especially pleases God.

11. And [Peter] saw heaven opened and an object like a
great sheet bound at the four corners, descending to him
and let down to the earth. 12. In it were all kinds of four-
footed animals of the earth, wild beasts, creeping things, and
birds of the air. 13. And a voice came to him, "Rise, Peter;
kill and eat." 14. But Peter said, "Not so, Lord! For I have
never eaten anything common or unclean." 15. And a voice
spoke to him again the second time, "What God has
cleansed you must not call common." 16. This was done
three times. And the object was taken up into heaven again.

We need to be reminded that Peter was not a Christian. He
did not even know the word "Christian" at this point in time. He

was a Jew, albeit a Messianic Jew. He was born again but he still behaved the way his mother and father had taught him. He faithfully kept the Jewish law. One thing Peter's mother had taught him was never to enter a Gentile house, and he probably had never previously violated this rule.

When Peter was with Jesus, he saw the Master minister to a Gentile Syro-Phoenician woman's daughter (see Mark 7:24-30) and a Roman centurion's servant (see Matt. 8:5-13). Neither of these, however, changed the inbred behavior of Peter, or of any of the other apostles for that matter. Peter had visited the great ingathering of Samaritans initiated by Philip, and he had approved of the legitimacy of "Messianic Samaritans." That was indeed a significant milestone, but in doing this he had not violated any part of the Jewish law.

It is hard for us today to understand just how revolting to Peter, or to any Orthodox Jew of that day, would be the thought of entering a Gentile home, particularly risking coming into contact with unclean food. Someone has said that a social situation that approaches it today might be the prejudice that high-caste Hindus have against low-caste Hindus. For Peter even to consider such a thing would be for him an enormously difficult decision.

To make it worse, none of the other apostles to whom Peter was accountable were there with him. If Peter could have consulted with someone such as John or James and have had at least one other agree with him it would have been much safer. But deciding on his own would entail a great risk. If the others didn't agree when they found out, irreparable damage could be done to the young church.

In light of this, God knew that ordinary communication processes would not be adequate to move Peter in the radical direction He wanted him to go. So God did an extraordinary thing and gave Peter the famous vision of the unclean food in the sheet. Peter's background had personally prepared him to receive visions. For one thing, it would fit his worldview. Unlike many today, Peter believed that one of God's normal ways of communicating from time to time was through visions and dreams. He was praying at the time, so his heart was open to God. He may have been fasting, too. Luke doesn't say he was, but we read that Peter **became very hungry** (Acts 10:10). Prayer along with fasting removes obstacles to hearing the voice of God.

Why would God choose Peter for this task and not Paul? Paul was the one who would be the career E-3 missionary to the Gentiles, not Peter, who later goes down in history as the apostle to the circumcision. The answer, I think, is straightforward. To establish unequivocally the bedrock, theological principle that the gospel was for the Gentiles as well as for the Jews, no less than one of the original 12 apostles needed to receive the revelation from God and the accompanying personal experience. God was preparing Peter, not to be a career missionary to the Gentiles, but rather, to give the right word at the right time in the Council of Jerusalem many years later. Furthermore, of all the 12 apostles, Peter was probably the greatest risk taker.

Unclean Food

Leviticus 11 lists "the animals which you may eat" (Lev. 11:2) and those "you shall not eat" (Lev. 11:4). Every Jew had been trained in this list from infancy. The language of the law is strong. For example, it says, "You shall not make yourselves abominable with any creeping thing that creeps; nor shall you make yourselves unclean with them, lest you be defiled by them" (Lev. 11:43). No Jew went around fighting the temptation to eat a ham sandwich or rabbit stew or steamed clams—the very thought of eating such things was nauseating. As a part of my missionary lifestyle, I eat just about anything. But I must admit, I think I would have a hard time among the Masai in Kenya if they offered me one of their delicacies, milk mixed with cow's blood. The Jews thought the same about eating a filthy pig.

The Jews weren't allowed to *touch* unclean food. They could drink milk, but not if it had been milked from the cow by a Gentile. They couldn't eat sheep if it had not been slaughtered by a rabbi and certified as kosher food.

The sheet God lowered in front of Peter was filled with all this unclean food and much more. When God said, **"Rise, Peter; kill and eat,"** (Acts 10:13) these must have been the most shocking words Peter had heard since Jesus told him years ago He would die and Peter would betray Him. Peter's knee-jerk reaction this time was the same as then: **"Not so, Lord!"** (10:14). Just to make sure no miscommunication had occurred, God then added, **"What God has cleansed you must not call common,"** (10:15) and repeated the vision twice more.

Peter did not instantly comprehend the meaning and the implications of the vision he had seen.

Cornelius's Party Arrives

17. ...the men who had been sent from Cornelius had made inquiry for Simon's house, and stood before the gate. 18. And they called and asked whether Simon, whose sur-name was Peter, was lodging there.

Meanwhile, Peter was still alone, processing what he had seen and heard. Events were moving rapidly. Again, to minimize any possibility that Peter would respond incorrectly, the Holy Spirit spoke directly to Peter a second time:

19. While Peter thought about the vision, the Spirit said to him, "Behold, three men are seeking you. 20. Arise

> therefore, go down and go with them, doubting nothing;
> for I have sent them."

God was moving Peter one step farther. Not only did He want to adjust Peter's aversion to unclean food, but now God also wanted Peter to realize he was to associate with unclean *people*. The three at the gate were three Gentiles!

> 21. Then Peter went down to the men who had been sent to him from Cornelius, and said, "Yes, I am he whom you seek. For what reason have you come?" 22. And they said, "Cornelius the centurion, a just man, one who fears God and has a good reputation among all the nation of the Jews, was divinely instructed by a holy angel to summon you to his house, and to hear words from you."

Because of the power of the vision Peter had received and the incredible divine synchronization of the timing of these interlocked events, Peter was thoroughly prepared to begin moving in the direction he now had understood God was taking him. In light of this, the next phrase is highly significant:

> 23. Then he invited them in and lodged them....

No self-respecting Orthodox Jews would, on the spur of the moment, invite three uncircumcised Gentile strangers into their houses, particularly at mealtime. But Peter invited them for one reason: God had told him to. The Romans would have had no problem eating the kosher food served in Simon the tanner's house, but it was in all probability the first time they themselves had been invited into a Jewish house and perhaps their first authentic kosher meal. They stayed overnight as well.

The problem would have been all on the Jewish side. In taking this risk, Peter was making the first small move into what would be a major turning point in the history of Christianity. The bigger risk was yet to come, for entertaining the Gentiles, as F. F. Bruce says, "did not expose him to such a risk of defilement as would a Jew's acceptance of hospitality in a Gentile's house."[8]

Peter Steps over the Line

> 23. ...On the next day Peter went away with them, and some brethren from Joppa accompanied him.
> 11:12. ...Moreover these six brethren accompanied me,....

Peter took a team of six other believers with him so that whatever happened would be attested by reliable witnesses. Furthermore, the others, particularly if intercessors were among them, would provide welcome on-site prayer support for the extraordinary ministry to which God had called Peter.

> 10:24. And the following day they entered Caesarea. Now Cornelius was waiting for them, and had called together his relatives and close friends. 25. As Peter was coming in, Cornelius met him and fell down at his feet and worshiped him. 26. But Peter lifted him up, saying, "Stand up; I myself am also a man."

Cornelius displayed his theological ignorance by attempting to worship Peter. But at the same time, he displayed his openness to whatever Peter had for him because by then he was sure it would be from God.

Undoubtedly many people had gathered in Cornelius's home. While the others were listening, Peter and Cornelius debriefed each other on their divinely synchronized visions, and the ice was broken.

The 10 verses Luke provides here are probably only a brief summary of all that Peter said to the group gathered in Cornelius's home.

34. Then Peter opened his mouth and said: "In truth I perceive that God shows no partiality. 35. But in every nation whoever fears Him and works righteousness is accepted by Him. 36. The word which God sent to the children of Israel, preaching peace through Jesus Christ— He is Lord of all— 37. that word you know, which was proclaimed throughout all Judea, and began from Galilee after the baptism which John preached: 38. how God anointed Jesus of Nazareth with the Holy Spirit and with power, who went about doing good and healing all who were oppressed by the devil, for God was with him. 39. "And we are witnesses of all things which He did both in the land of the Jews and in Jerusalem, whom they killed by hanging on a tree. 40. Him God raised up on the third day, and showed Him openly, 41. not to all the people, but to witnesses chosen before by God, even to us who ate and drank with Him after He arose from the dead. 42. "And He commanded us to preach to the people, and to testify that it is He who was ordained by God to be Judge of the living and the dead. 43. To Him all the prophets witness that, through His name, whoever believes in Him will receive remission of sins."

Peter's introductory words say it all: **God shows no partiality.** Cornelius and the rest of the people in his house were ready to believe that God was going to save them. Peter summarized the chief elements of the gospel in his message, but at one point he targeted it specifically to the Gentiles: **"whom they killed by hanging on a tree."** This focuses on the action of nailing Jesus to the cross, which Roman soldiers, such as those under Cornelius's command, performed. When Peter preached to Jews, he did not stress the act of *nailing* Jesus to the cross, but rather the *accusations* against Jesus that ultimately led to crucifixion (see Acts 2:23). In short, we all, both Jews and Gentiles, share the blame for Jesus' death and, therefore, we need to repent.

This is a somewhat elementary, but nevertheless real, example of what missiologists call "contextualizing" the gospel. It doesn't change the gospel message, but it does change the way it is tailored to a variety of audiences who have a wide array of felt needs. We will see much more radical examples of this when we study the missionary experiences of the apostle Paul.

Pentecost—Phase III

As I commented on Acts 2 in the first volume of this series, *Spreading the Fire*, I suggested that we do well to regard Pentecost, or the coming of the Holy Spirit in power, as a three-phase event. Each phase marks a significant cross-cultural advance of the gospel. Phase I is in Acts 2 where the gospel crossed the barrier between Hebrew Jews and Hellenistic Jews. Phase II is in Acts 8 where the barrier was broken between Jews and Samaritans. And this is Phase III where the gospel moves across the cultural chasm between Jews and Gentiles.

Note that Peter was involved personally in all three of these phases. In Matthew 16:19, Jesus tells Peter that as a spokesperson for the rest, He would give him the keys of the kingdom of heaven in order to build His Church. It could be that what we see here are three high-profile uses of those keys.

The ministry of the power of the Holy Spirit in Cornelius's house was awesome. Peter never had a chance to finish his message:

> **10:44.** While Peter was still speaking these words, the
> Holy Spirit fell upon all those who heard the word.

From Luke's report, it seems as though Peter experienced a clean evangelistic sweep. All the unbelievers present were apparently saved. Luke does not list all of the visible manifestations of the Holy Spirit in that meeting, but he stresses the one that attracted the most attention:

> **45.** And those of the circumcision who believed were
> astonished, as many as came with Peter, because the gift
> of the Holy Spirit had been poured out on the Gentiles
> also. **46.** For they heard them speak with tongues and
> magnify God....

While the gift of tongues in Pentecost Phase I (Acts 2) was specifically intended for the proclamation of the gospel to representatives of the many ethnic groups present in Jerusalem at that time, the gift of tongues here in Cornelius's house seems more intended to be a confirmation of the validity of these initial Gentile conversions. Speaking in tongues, in this particular case the initial physical evidence of the filling of the Holy Spirit, was sufficient for Peter to order baptism immediately:

> **10:47.** "Can anyone forbid water, that these should not be
> baptized who have received the Holy Spirit just as we
> have?" **48.** And he commanded them to be baptized in the
> name of the Lord....

Although Luke doesn't mention it, it is important to note that the matter of circumcision does not surface. As we will see when we move ahead toward the Jerusalem Council, this is an enormously significant issue, the key point in affirming the validity of cross-cultural missionary work to the Gentiles.

Peter Is in Big Trouble
Acts 11

As he would have anticipated, Peter's most formidable challenge was just ahead. How would he report what he had just done to his Orthodox Jewish apostolic colleagues who had not seen the vision of the animals in the sheet and who had not been in Cornelius's house when the Holy Spirit fell with power?

11:2. And when Peter came up to Jerusalem, those of the circumcision contended with him, 3. saying, "You went in to uncircumcised men and ate with them!"

The leaders of the Jerusalem church were furious. They were not particularly ready to hear Peter say words to the effect, "I went to Cornelius's house and ate with Gentiles because God told me to." Much as they believed that God does speak directive words to individual people, they needed more than that to assimilate this one. They were shocked!

Who are **those of the circumcision**? Biblical scholars do not agree whether a conservative group of Messianic Jews who continued to insist that Gentiles be circumcised as a prerequisite for being a disciple of Jesus Christ had begun to form in Jerusalem this early. By Acts 15, however, the conservative Messianic Jews were in full operation, teaching: **"Unless you are circumcised according to the custom of Moses, you cannot be saved"** (v. 1). But here, perhaps, those of the circumcision only means Jewish believers in general. Whatever the meaning, they were extremely upset with Peter.

Peter defended his activities by describing his ministry experience rather than arguing theology. Chances are that at this time he wouldn't have worked out a cogent theology to explain what he had just seen firsthand. Once again I will point out that, as we see in most of the subsequent history of Christianity, theology emerges from ministry, not vice versa.

Peter's most convincing point was that the new Gentile believers in Caesarea had spoken in tongues. He says:

> 17. "If therefore God gave them the same gift as He gave us when we believed on the Lord Jesus Christ, who was I that I could withstand God?"

The power of the Holy Spirit must have fallen strongly on the group in Jerusalem who had at first criticized Peter so severely, because in response to his simple testimony their anger turned to silence and then to approval.

> 18. When they heard these things they became silent; and they glorified God, saying, "Then God has also granted to the Gentiles repentance to life."

Peter's Tremendous Victory

To summarize, Peter concluded a relatively short assignment to cross-cultural ministry by experiencing a tremendous victory. Although he did not have the ongoing spiritual gift of missionary, he served God from his role as an obedient servant. We ourselves do many things from our roles as faithful Christians although we might not have the gift for a more permanent ministry in those roles. For example, I have led people to Christ although I don't have the gift of evangelist; I have cast out demons although I don't have the gift of deliverance; I have prophesied although I don't have the gift of prophecy. On the other hand, I serve Fuller Seminary and I write books, not out of a role, but because God has given me the spiritual gift of teaching.

Paul is the one who emerges as having a strong gift of missionary. As we will see in more detail later, Peter makes some serious mistakes when he attempts to minister to the first Gentile church in Antioch. God had anointed Peter as the apostle to the circumcision, but when called upon to break the Gentile barrier in the house of Cornelius, he rose to the occasion, ministered to the uncircumcision and turned a key to the Kingdom that has seen multiplied benefits through the centuries.

Reflection Questions

1. The concept of "people movements," involving the members of a whole group making a decision to accept Christ all at once, is foreign to most of us. Do you think it is valid? What would be its dangers?

2. How could it be that some committed Christians who believe Peter raised Dorcas from the dead doubt that the dead are being raised today?

3. Proselytes and God-fearers were both born Gentiles. How did they differ from each other? What difference would it make in their receptivity to the gospel? NINE

4. Obviously, God's choice of Cornelius to lead the first notable conversion of Gentiles was a deliberate choice. What were the two or three principal reasons God would have chosen Cornelius as opposed to any one of hundreds of other Gentiles?

5. Of all the things that persuaded Peter he should violate Jewish law and enter the house of a Gentile such as Cornelius, which do you think could have been the most important? The Vision + word from God

Notes

1. C. Peter Wagner, *Church Planting for a Greater Harvest* (Ventura, CA: Regal Books, 1990), p. 11.
2. C. Peter Wagner, *Your Spiritual Gifts Can Help Your Church Grow* (Ventura, CA: Regal Books, 1979; revised edition, 1994), p. 179.
3. Donald A. McGavran, *Understanding Church Growth* (Grand Rapids: William B. Eerdmans Publishing Co., 1970; 1980; third edition revised and edited by C. Peter Wagner, 1990), p. 241.
4. Ibid., p. 227.
5. Carl Lawrence, *The Church in China* (Minneapolis: Bethany House Publishers, 1985), pp. 76-77.
6. F. F. Bruce, *The Book of Acts* (Grand Rapids: William B. Eerdmans Publishing Co., 1954; revised edition, 1988), p. 58.
7. John Stott, *The Spirit, the Church and the World: The Message of Acts* (Downers Grove, IL: InterVarsity Press, 1990), p. 185.
8. Bruce, *The Book of Acts*, p. 208.

Planting the First Gentile Church

Peter blazed the trail, and by baptizing Cornelius, and Cornelius's family and friends, he laid the foundation for all future ministry among the Gentiles of the world. As soon as Luke finishes his account of this event, which as I mentioned, is the longest story in the book of Acts, he then tells how the first Gentile church was planted. It was not to be planted in Cornelius's city of Caesarea, but rather in Antioch of Syria.

The Big Picture

As we frequently do, let's once again take a look at the big picture of the book of Acts. Our guiding light is Acts 1:8:

1:8. But you shall receive power when the Holy Spirit has come upon you; and you shall be witnesses to Me in

Jerusalem, and in all Judea and Samaria, and to the
end of the earth.

....

My rationale for writing this commentary on Acts is to expand
on the two themes of this verse—missiology and power ministry—more than other commentaries have done.

Missiologically, three broad cultural groups are highlighted in
Acts 1:8: Jews, Samaritans and Gentiles. From this perspective,
the entire book of Acts can be outlined around the three groups:

• Part I deals with church growth in Jerusalem and Judea.
Evangelism is directed mostly at the Jews, and Peter is the central figure. This covers Acts 1—6.

• Part II deals with church growth in Samaria. Stephen and
Philip are the central figures, Stephen being the theoretician and
Philip the practitioner. This covers Acts 6—8.

• Part III deals with church growth among the Gentiles. Paul
becomes the central figure, and this is by far Luke's largest
emphasis, covering Acts 9—28, or more than two-thirds of the
book. To lead in, Luke introduces Paul (see Acts 9), tells how
Peter blazed the trail to Cornelius's house (see Acts 9—11), tran-
sitions from Peter to Paul (see Acts 11—12) and then spotlights
Paul's ministry for the rest of the book (see Acts 13—28).

As indicated in Acts 1:8, this cross-cultural advance of the
kingdom of God would be characterized by the supernatural
power of the Holy Spirit working through the disciples. Luke
highlights this in Part I by the miracle of tongues or languages in
Act 2:4, and **many signs and wonders** in 2:43, 4:30 and 5:12.

In Part II, Stephen **did great wonders and signs among the people** (6:8) and **multitudes with one accord heeded the things spoken by Philip, hearing and seeing the miracles which he did** (8:6).

Now, as we move into Part III, we have already seen Peter
healing Aeneas and raising Dorcas from the dead. Such power

ministries will continue with Paul and Barnabas later **declaring how many miracles and wonders God had worked through them among the Gentiles** (15:12).

Believers Were Persecuted, But They Evangelized

> **11:19.** Now those who were scattered after the persecution that arose over Stephen....

To refresh our memories, Stephen had delivered a powerful message to the Sanhedrin, suggesting that God could save people apart from the Temple in Jerusalem and apart from the Jewish law. It cost him his life. None other than Paul, then called Saul, took leadership of the explosive persecution that followed this event, and the believers were scattered. To review:

> **8:3.** As for Saul, he made havoc of the church, entering every house, and dragging off men and women, committing them to prison. **4.** Therefore those who were scattered went everywhere preaching the word.

The same passage states:

> **8:1.** ...they were all scattered throughout the regions of Judea and Samaria, except the apostles.

The phrase **except the apostles** indicates that it was not the *Hebrew* Jewish believers, but the *Hellenistic* Jewish believers who had been driven out of Jerusalem. The church split between the two groups was described in Acts 6 where the apostles decided to appoint the seven leaders of the Hellenistic church.

We need to keep in mind that when these Hellenistic believers traveled through the region witnessing and planting churches, the churches they planted did not take the form we are accustomed to today. The believers had no separate Christian church buildings where they met. They were Jews and they continued worshiping God on Saturdays in the synagogues. When they met with other believers or Messianic Jews for fellowship, prayer, worship or the Lord's Supper, it was in homes. The Greek word for church, *ekklesia*, simply means "assembly," "gathering" or "congregation." It did not mean a church building nor did it carry many other of the institutional implications the word "church" does today. Nor did it mean the synagogue. It is notable that the early Jewish believers tended to avoid using the word "synagogue" for their assemblies.

Church planting, then, meant to proclaim the gospel in word and deed, and to gather those who believed into fellowship groups, meeting in any number of homes. Those in a given city who were called followers of Jesus Christ were the church in that particular city.

When, beginning in Antioch, churches that were essentially composed of Gentiles came into being, a new dimension of the church began. These Gentile believers, by and large, had no reason to worship in the synagogue on the Sabbath. But this development comes later. As the Hellenistic Jews went out from Jerusalem, they did not preach to Gentiles, but to Jews only, as the second part of Acts 11:19 says:

> 19. Now those who were scattered after the persecution that arose over Stephen traveled as far as Phoenicia, Cyprus, and Antioch, preaching the word to no one but the Jews only.

Geographically, the scattered believers headed west from Jerusalem and turned right at the Mediterranean Sea. Luke mentions three places in particular, but we have no reason to doubt that they might have evangelized Jews living in other places as well. The three places specifically mentioned are:

Phoenicia. Phoenicia was a province beginning just north of Galilee, having three principal cities in the Mediterranean: Ptolemais, Tyre and Sidon. In Acts 21, we are later told that the disciples were at Tyre (see vv. 3,4) and Ptolemais (see v. 7). We would be safe to assume that some disciples had gone to Sidon also, and that all three of these churches were planted by the fleeing Hellenists.

Cyprus. Cyprus was a large island a little more than 100 miles from the mainland. Some believers might have gone there from Sidon by sea. Two major cities were located in Cyprus: Salamis in the east and Paphos in the west. The church, or churches, on Cyprus fairly rapidly became missionary-sending churches because we read in Acts 11:20 that missionaries went from Cyprus to Antioch.

Antioch. Antioch was the capital of Syria. In the Roman Empire, only Rome and Alexandria were larger cities, so Antioch was a highly important and strategic center. The population of Antioch at that time is estimated by some to be 500,000. It was not on the coast, but about 20 miles inland on the Orontes River. Antioch is now in Turkey and carries the name Antakya. When Rome conquered Syria in 64 B.C., Pompey designated Antioch as a free city and made it the capital of western Asia. The city was favored with majestic architecture and beautifully paved streets. It was an important commercial center through which the goods and produce of the regions to the east found their way to the shipping routes of the Mediterranean.

Antioch had an exceptionally large Jewish population. F. F.

Bruce says, "Jewish colonization in Antioch began practically from the city's foundation."[1] That means Jews had been living there for some 300 years. Some have estimated Antioch's Jewish population to be 25,000 at the time of the events in the book of Acts. As was customary, the Jews would have resided in a special section of the city called "the Jewish quarter." The Jews in Antioch are said to have been more aggressive and more successful in proselytizing Gentiles than most. When the seven Hellenistic leaders were appointed by the apostles in Acts 6, one was **Nicolas, a proselyte from Antioch** (v. 5).

The Gentile part of Antioch had fallen into moral degradation. Simon Kistemaker says, "Antioch was known not for its virtues but for its vices: it was a city of moral depravity."[2] This would have been, to a large extent, because of the spiritual captivity of many in the city to the demonic principalities of Artemis (Diana of the Ephesians) and Apollo. Their center of worship was located in the nearby suburb of Daphene, where ritual prostitution drew its crowds. W. J. Conybeare and J. S. Howson describe Daphene as "a sanctuary for a perpetual festival of vice."[3]

I have spent some time in describing the city of Antioch because from this point in history it begins to rise in importance as the center of early Christianity on a par with Jerusalem. It is the place where the first Gentile church, in the proper sense of the word, was to be established.

The Mission to Antioch's Jews

Meanwhile, the Hellenists who left Jerusalem under the persecution had planted the first church in Antioch. But it was a church planted among Jews, not among Gentiles. This is an example of what we have been calling E-1, or monocultural, evangelism. From the missiological perspective, the geographical distance covered in an evangelistic effort is secondary compared to the cultural distance. I recall missiologist Ralph Winter once saying that the first thousand miles are insignificant when compared to the last three feet!

In this case, the Hellenistic believers would have traveled 300 miles or so from Jerusalem to Antioch, a considerable distance in those days. But when they arrived in Antioch, they would have taken up residence in the Jewish quarter of the city and established their primary social relationships among the Jewish people. They would inevitably have had some social contact with Gentiles in such a cosmopolitan city, but such contacts would be marginal as far as personal relationships were concerned. They would not have eaten with Gentiles, invited them into their Jewish homes or gone out of their way to share the gospel of Jesus Christ with them. This is why Luke specifically says they were **preaching the word to no one but the Jews only** (11:19).

If some may have difficulty imagining this, a modern parallel would be the evangelization of the Korean immigrant population in Los Angeles in the 1980s and 1990s. So many Koreans came that a section of Los Angeles was designated "Koreatown," similar to the Jewish quarter in Antioch except that many more Koreans reside in Los Angeles than Jews in Antioch. Pastors and evangelists came to Los Angeles from Korea in considerable numbers to evangelize the Koreans, and they had outstanding success. In Korea itself, some 25 percent of the population are Christian, but in Los Angeles the number of Christians among first-generation Korean-Americans is reported at nearly 70 percent!

Most of this evangelism in Los Angeles was successful because it was also E-1 evangelism. When the Korean pastors arrived in Los Angeles, they found people who spoke the same language, ate the same food, harbored the same prejudices, married the same kind of people, honored their ancestors in the same way and shared many other common interests. We might say that these pastors and evangelists from Korea "preached the word to none but Koreans only."

It could be pointed out, having a good deal of validity, that Los Angeles Korean-Americans are somewhat different from Korean-Koreans. The same would have been true of Hellenistic Jews in Antioch as compared to Hellenistic Jews in Jerusalem. It could be argued that they should be seen as distinct people groups, and in that case the evangelism would be E-2 rather than E-1. This might be true, but it simply illustrates that a bit of subjectivity is inevitably involved in discerning boundaries between some people groups. This is why, at the present time, some missiologists will say that 6,000 people groups are still unreached in the world while others will say the amount is 12,000. The issue is not right or wrong but a matter of subjective personal judgment.

The major point here in Acts 11, however, is that these Hellenists from Jerusalem did not preach to the *Gentiles* in Antioch any more than the Korean evangelists in Los Angeles would have preached to the non-Korean Anglo-Americans, African-Americans or Hispanic-Americans. Add to this the Japanese-Americans toward whom modern-day Koreans harbor feelings similar to the feelings of Jews toward Gentiles in the first century.

Two Missions to Antioch, Not One

....

20. But some of them were men from Cyprus and Cyrene, who, when they had come to Antioch, spoke to the Hellenists [Gentiles], preaching the Lord Jesus. 21. And the hand of the Lord was with them, and a great number believed and turned to the Lord.

....

Were there in fact *two* mission advances into the city of Antioch instead of *one*? Was the first mission undertaken by the Hellenistic Jewish sisters and brothers who left Jerusalem after Stephen's death and the second by a group of unrelated missionaries? Did one target the Jewish population of Antioch and the other the Gentile population? Were there several years between the first arrival of each group?

This is a particularly important question for missiologists, especially for those who have a high view of culture and believe that the people approach to world evangelization has been, and still is, the most viable strategy for planning and executing crosscultural evangelism. Because I am one who tends to interpret missionary work from such a perspective, my conclusion is that to most accurately understand the information Luke provides in Acts 11, a two-mission hypothesis is useful.

I am well aware of the risk I am taking in suggesting this. None of the respected commentators I have been consulting throughout my study of Acts proposes that two separate missions occurred. At the same time, none of them rejects the idea, apparently because such a hypothesis has not yet been raised as a point of discussion among biblical scholars.

Almost all of the commentators, however, pause with no small frustration at this point, trying to make a coherent whole out of the bits and pieces of information Luke provides. Howard Marshall says, "There can be no doubt that a successful period of evangelism among Gentiles was initiated....What we do not know is how the church was led to take this step."[4] Simon Kistemaker says, "We are unable to explain why Jewish people from Cyrene in North Africa came to Antioch."[5] F. F. Bruce says, "But in Antioch some daring spirits among them, men of Cyprus and Cyrene, took a momentous step forward. If the gospel was so good for the Jews, might it not be good for the Gentiles also?"[6]

Although they do not wrestle specifically with the two-mission hypothesis, the biblical scholars do discuss extensively two other important items in this passage. One is whether it makes the best sense to conclude that planting the church among the Gentiles in Antioch came *before* the conversion of Cornelius or *after*. In my opinion, and that of most of the commentators I am using, there are no substantial reasons to change the order Luke uses in the Acts of the Apostles. Cornelius came first, then the Gentiles in Antioch.

A much more crucial issue from the viewpoint of missiology is who these people called "Hellenists" in *The New King James Version*, the version I am using, really are. Some of the ancient Greek texts use *Hellenas* or "Greeks," while others use *Hellenistas* or "Hellenists." Simon Kistemaker sums it up well: "[Luke] intimates that the Jewish Christian missionaries addressed not the Greek-speaking Jews, whom he elsewhere calls *Hellenists*, but the non-Jewish Greeks, whom he repeatedly classifies as *Hellenas*. The internal evidence, therefore, seems to favor the reading *Greeks*."[7]

When I quoted Acts 11:20 on a previous page, I inserted the word "Gentiles," i.e., **they...spoke to the Hellenists [Gentiles]**. Who were these Gentiles? This is a secondary issue but an interesting one. R. C. H. Lenski points out, "Luke omits any further characterization such as used in connection with Cornelius in 10:2, to the effect that they were 'fearing God.'"[8] An argument from silence proves nothing for sure but it does indicate that we cannot be certain whether these Gentiles were, in fact, God-fearers or whether they were other Gentiles who had no connection with the Jewish synagogues whatsoever. There could have been some of each for all we know.

The CCM (Cyprus and Cyrene Mission)

My personal reconstruction of historical events has the Hellenistic believers leaving Jerusalem after Stephen's death and planting solid, growing churches in both Cyprus and Cyrene as well as many other places. Luke explicitly tells us they went to Cyprus (see 11:19), although he does not mention Cyrene. We have no reason, however, to doubt that they went to Cyrene as well. In another place Luke says, **those who were scattered went everywhere preaching the word** (8:4), so everywhere could well have included Cyrene. Cyrene was a city in North Africa, now Libya.

Let's assume, then, that the churches that were planted in Cyrene and Cyprus developed satisfactorily over the years, and that they eventually became missionary-sending churches, as healthy churches should. Charles Van Engen argues that by their very nature, true disciples of Jesus are "God's missionary people,"[9] and I do not think it is unreasonable to expect that these first-century believers would have been anything different.

Because these believers were still Jews, and had been Jews all their lives, they would have been familiar with what we have mentioned previously as the Jewish proselytizing bands. Jesus referred to these bands in passing when He said of the Pharisees: "For you travel land and sea to win one proselyte" (Matt. 23:15). The proselytizing bands functioned apart from the local synagogues as, what missiologists call, "sodalities," roughly equivalent to what we know as "parachurch organizations" today.

It is altogether possible that believers from both Cyprus and Cyrene who had the spiritual gift of missionary had joined forces to establish what would be to us a parachurch missionary agency. This is exactly what we will see Paul, Barnabas and some others doing when we come to Acts 13. There is no need to think they were the first ones to do it, they are just the ones about whom we know the most. When we come to Acts 13, I will explain the so-called "modality-sodality theory" in more detail.

If these proselytizing bands did do church planting, let's call it the "Cyprus and Cyrene Mission," or the "CCM," just to coin a term for communication purposes.

When Did the CCM Arrive in Antioch?

Biblical scholars do not agree on how the chronology of Acts falls into place at several points. It is a complex matter, and the arguments on all sides are readily available to any who desire to consult the classical commentaries. In the first chapter of Book 1 of this series on Acts, *Spreading the Fire*, I discussed the chronology and set out my own conclusions in a time line that seems to me to be the most reasonable way of interpreting all the facts we have. I have also included it in the introductory pages of this book. For this discussion about when the CCM arrived in Antioch and began to plant Gentile churches, I am following that time line chronology.

As we will see later in Acts 11, Paul was called to Antioch in A.D. 46, fairly soon after the Gentile churches had been planted there. It is a judgment call, but I would think this would be three or four years, at the most, after the CCM missionaries first arrived. This would put the arrival of the CCM at A.D. 42 or 43, possibly a little later.

That was Mission Number 2, but how about Mission Number 1? Stephen's death and the persecution that scattered the Hellenistic believers occurred in A.D. 32, the year before Saul's conversion in A.D. 33. We do not know how long it took these Hellenistic Jewish missionaries to begin to plant churches in the Jewish ghetto of Antioch, but it was probably not more than a year or two at the most.

One more thing. Soon after Paul arrived and began to minister in Antioch, the believers there took up an offering and sent it to the church in Jerusalem, which at the time was suffering from a famine (see 11:27-30). In Galatians, Paul says he and

Barnabas took that offering 14 years after he made the short visit from Damascus to Jerusalem following his conversion (see Gal. 2:1). How the 14 years might exactly fit the sequence of events is part of the ongoing scholarly discussion on chronology, but not particularly relevant to my point here.

My point is that, based on these facts, *several years elapsed, perhaps 8 or 10, between the time of the first mission to the Jews of Antioch and the second mission to the Gentiles of Antioch.*

What Did the CCM Do?

Let's try to reconstruct the scenario in Antioch as a missiologist might see it. Here is Antioch, a cosmopolitan city of 500,000. William LaSor says, "The city was divided into 'quarters,' and had a large Jewish population, as well as Syrian, Greek, and Roman communities."[10] From this, we know that it comprised at least four people groups, undoubtedly many more. But working from the information we have, we can meaningfully discuss only the two broader people groups, the Jews and the Gentiles.

The Jewish population, as we have previously mentioned, consisted of 25,000 people. This is a large number of Jews, as LaSor says, but it is only 5 percent of the total population of Antioch. Antioch also had 475,000 Gentiles when the CCM arrived to evangelize them.

When the CCM missionaries got to Antioch they found a well-established church, about 10 years old, in the Jewish quarter. The believers there were seen by themselves, and by the other residents of Antioch, as minority Jews who worshiped in the synagogues, kept a kosher kitchen, considered uncircumcised Gentiles as unclean and followed Jesus Christ as their Messiah. Luke has told us specifically that these people were **preaching the word to no one but the Jews only** (Acts 11:19). They were making no attempt, that we are aware of, to reach the 475,000

Gentiles in Antioch. Because of this, they were an unlikely force for evangelism to Antioch's unreached people groups.

Preaching to Gentiles Only

The CCM missionaries arrived with a different perspective. We might surmise that their calling from God was **preaching the word to no one but the [Gentiles] only.** They were intentionally cross-cultural. Unlike those in the Jewish quarter, they would likely have been given the missionary gift by the Holy Spirit. Although ethnically they were just as Jewish as those in the Jewish-quarter church, they were also significantly different from them. They came with an anointing of the Holy Spirit to communicate the gospel cross-culturally to the *Gentiles*.

Methodologically, they would not have wanted to be strongly associated with the believers in the Jewish quarter. Why? Although in a city as large as Antioch, the vast majority of citizens would not have known about such things as disciples of Jesus Christ in the Jewish quarter, those who did know would have seen them as extremely ethnocentric, not to say racist. The Messianic Jews would have taught that in order to worship God and enter their synagogues, Gentiles first would have to become Jews, be circumcised and agree to keep the Jewish law—at least the majority of them would be of that opinion. They would not as yet have absorbed the theological implications of Peter's visit to Cornelius's house. The theological principles behind the issue of Gentile circumcision continued to be poorly understood by Jewish believers at least until the Council of Jerusalem, which came several years after the first Gentile church was established.

The CCM missionaries had resolved the theological issue, at least to their satisfaction. They were prepared to evangelize the Gentiles on their own merits, not requiring them to become Jews to be saved. I can picture these missionaries not settling down in the Jewish quarter, but rather in the Syrian quarter, the Greek quarter or the Roman quarter in order to begin to multiply churches.

In a city so large and among people groups so distinct, I would not think the social contact between the network of house churches in the Jewish quarter and the new churches of the Gentile quarters would have been extensive, if they had any direct contact at all. Furthermore, considering their theological differences, a modern analogy might be picturing Assemblies of God missionaries going to evangelize the lower castes of a large Indian city where the Lutherans had been established among middle castes for many years. They would likely acknowledge each other as part of the general Christian church of the city, but working contacts would be minimal or, most likely, nonexistent. The one thing that might have brought them closer together would be persecution, but we do not read of persecution arising in Antioch.

The result would have been that a network of Syrian Gentile churches would have developed, and perhaps another network of Roman Gentile churches, and perhaps others, depending on how many of the specific Gentile people groups in Antioch the missionaries had targeted. These would have been as separate from each other as are the networks of Korean churches and Hispanic churches and African-American churches and Messianic Jewish synagogues in Los Angeles today. In a broad theological sense, they are all truly "the Church of Jesus Christ in Los Angeles," but functionally they see themselves as distinct from the others. What meaningful social interaction the Gentile and the Jewish churches in Antioch might have had is unknown. But if what we know about intercultural communication applied then as it does now, whatever social interaction they might have had with each other would have been a *secondary* social relationship. Their *primary* relationships would have been with fellow Jews or fellow Gentiles, as the case may be.

I realize that some will say such a reconstruction of the scenario in Antioch is not politically correct. They would prefer to postulate that Jewish believers and Gentile believers, whether Syrian, Greek, Roman or others, would all be worshiping together in the same assembly, eating together and intermarrying freely. I myself would also prefer this, because it would be a wonderful display of our oneness in Christ. I also would prefer that this be the case in Los Angeles or Calcutta or Mexico City or Kinchasa today. But such, unfortunately, is not usually so. It will happen in the New Jerusalem, and I can report that it is happening occasionally today where the values of the kingdom of God are strongly manifested. We should pray that it happens more often. But in the meantime, we need to be as realistic as possible and admit that through the centuries it has been the exception, not the rule. Knowing what we know about the pre-Jerusalem Council generation of Jewish believers, it is extremely doubtful that Antioch was one of the exceptions to the rule. The multinational group mentioned in Acts 13:1 does not disprove my hypothesis, as we shall see later.

The Outcome

....

11:21. And the hand of the Lord was with them, and a great number believed and turned to the Lord.

....

Great church growth resulted from the church-planting initiative of the Cyprus and Cyrene Mission. These were the first known Gentile churches. The conversions of the Ethiopian eunuch and those in Cornelius's house were prototypes of individual conversion, but they have not become examples of Gentile church planting. Antioch was the pioneer.

The great growth of the Gentile churches in Antioch was due primarily to the two strands we are following through the book of Acts: divine power and sound missiology. The missiology I have gone into in great detail, because this is a crucial hinge in the history of Christianity. But how about the power? Nothing is specifically mentioned here about healings or miracles or speaking in tongues.

Luke does say, however, that **the hand of the Lord was with them.** Stanley Horton points out, "This expression is often used in the Bible to mean the power of the Lord or even the Spirit of the Lord."[11] Luke himself mentions **the hand of the Lord** on two other occasions in Acts, both describing displays of supernatural power. One was in a prayer meeting in Jerusalem where the believers prayed that God would act **"by stretching out Your hand to heal, and that signs and wonders may be done through the name of Your holy Servant Jesus"** (4:30). The other comes during a high-level power encounter between Paul and Elymas the sorcerer. Paul declares: **"And now, indeed, the hand of the Lord is upon you, and you shall be blind, not seeing the sun for a time"** (13:11).

True to form, then, the CCM missionaries moved among the Gentiles in Antioch by using power ministries, all the more necessary because of the wicked influence of dark angels under such principalities as Artemis (Diana) and Apollo headquartered in nearby Daphene, which may well have been the seat of Satan for the region.

Barnabas Arrives to Speed Up the Growth

11:22. Then news of these things came to the ears of the church in Jerusalem, and they sent out Barnabas to go as far as Antioch. 23. When he came and had seen the grace

of God, he was glad, and encouraged them all that with
purpose of heart they should continue with the Lord.
24. For he was a good man, full of the Holy Spirit and of
faith. And a great many people were added to the Lord.

The news that attracted the attention of the leaders in Jerusalem
was that Gentile churches were being multiplied in Antioch. They
would have known about the Jewish-quarter churches for some 10
years, so that wouldn't have been news. They might have been
shocked at the notion of Gentile churches, except that Peter's experience in the house of Cornelius fortunately had broken the ice.

When they had heard the news that Samaritans were coming
to Christ through Philip, the church leaders at Jerusalem sent
Peter and John to assess the situation and help as they could.
They again followed the same pattern in Antioch by sending
Barnabas. Barnabas is later referred to as an apostle (see 14:4),
but whether he was so regarded at this point we are not sure. In
any case, he had become an outstanding leader in the Jerusalem
church. He was one of those who had sold his land and given the
money to the church (see 4:36), and he had taken Paul under his
wing when he first visited Jerusalem as a new convert and was
still subject to a great deal of suspicion (see 9:26,27).

When Barnabas was sent to Antioch it was as a career missionary, not as a short-term missionary as were Peter and John
when they visited Samaria. Barnabas had the missionary gift but
neither Peter nor John did; they were both apostles to the Jews.
Barnabas originally came from Cyprus, so he may have known
the CCM missionaries from there. Even if he had not known
them, at least they would have had much in common and have
had mutual friends. Barnabas was one of the Jewish believers, relatively few at that time, who could comfortably accept uncircumcised Gentiles into the church.

Somewhat uncharacteristically, Luke gives two church-growth reports in a row here. Before Barnabas arrived, **a great number believed and turned to the Lord** (11:21). When Barnabas had been there for a while, Luke says, three verses later, **And a great many people were added to the Lord.** Apparently, good growth became better growth. The *rate* of church growth had evidently increased as a result of Barnabas's ministry.

Why would this happen? One reason might be that Barnabas was an encourager, and he brought with him an affirmation of apostolic approval from Jerusalem. He was an outstanding leader, and leadership is a proven principle of vigorous church growth.

Another reason would be that Barnabas was said to be **full of the Holy Spirit and of faith** (11:24). This is Luke's way of affirming that Barnabas was operating under a strong anointing for power ministries. A similar thing had been said of Stephen, **a man full of faith and the Holy Spirit** (6:5), and then, **Stephen, full of faith and power, did great wonders and signs among the people** (v. 8). The faith Luke is referring to here is more than saving faith or sanctifying faith. It is the extraordinary faith that believes for the miraculous, the faith Paul refers to in 1 Corinthians 13 to "remove mountains" (v. 2). Barnabas would later report with Paul **how many miracles and wonders God had worked through them among the Gentiles** (Acts 15:12). If power ministries are seen not so much as ends in themselves but as signs pointing to the Savior, a frequent outcome is that **a great many people...[are] added to the Lord** (11:24).

Paul Arrives to Train Leaders

25. Then Barnabas departed for Tarsus to seek Saul.
26. And when he had found him, he brought him to

> Antioch. So it was that for a whole year they assembled
> with the church and taught a great many people....

Why Barnabas invited Paul to join the large rapidly growing
Christian community in Antioch, Luke leaves largely to our
imagination. I would think he had two principal reasons:

1. As in any people movement, *training leaders is the major key
to success or failure.* Many of us are accustomed to hearing, at
times, reports of enormous numbers of people registering decisions for Christ at citywide evangelistic crusades, but finding few
of them moving ahead as committed Christians a year later.
Careful studies have shown that the major defect in strategy
planning (not the only one, to be sure) has been the failure to
select and train leaders. In the major hot growth spots of the
world today, the desperate need is not for missionaries to come
and evangelize—that is already happening in a remarkable way.
The need is for missionaries who are principally church planters
to come and train leaders. Without the concomitant multiplication of churches, evangelistic fruit will not be fruit that remains.

Luke does tell us that Paul **taught a great many people,** so
leadership training was evidently a part of Paul's job description.

But why Paul? He was not the only one who by that time
could train leaders and church planters. Furthermore, Paul had
practically disappeared from sight during the 10 years or so since
he had been strongly encouraged by the apostles to get out of
Jerusalem and go back home to Tarsus. It also helps to remind
ourselves that at that time Paul was not the famous Christian
leader we now know. Barnabas had a much higher profile and a
much greater name recognition.

What had Paul been doing for those 10 years? He tells us in
Galatians, "I went into the regions of Syria and Cilicia" (Gal.
1:21). Antioch was in this general territory, as well as Tarsus,

although they were several days' journey apart. We later hear of churches in Syria and Cilicia (see Acts 15:23), but we do not know if they were planted by Paul or by others.

It is not sure to what extent Paul, who was a Hebrew of the Hebrews and of the strict sect of the Pharisees, had at this point absorbed the theology that Gentiles could be saved without being circumcised. Paul's theology of Jesus as the true Messiah was firm. He had known since his experience on the Damascus road that God was calling him to minister to Gentiles. But how well he was prepared for this ministry remains a question.

This leads me to what I believe is the second, and perhaps most important, reason that Barnabas, under the leading of the Holy Spirit, invited Paul to come to Antioch from Tarsus.

2. *Paul came to Tarsus, not only to teach, but to learn.* If the hypothesis that theology emerges from ministry is valid, a year's ministry experience in a growing network of Gentile churches would have been an invaluable theological crucible. Paul would have been in the midst of possibly thousands of Gentiles, who by then were born again and serving Christ in a variety of roles in the church without having been circumcised or committed to following the Jewish law.

I would not be surprised if the compelling reason Barnabas set out to seek the relatively unknown Saul of Tarsus to recruit him for the missionary team in Antioch would be traced back to some revelatory word from God to the Antioch leaders. God's time had now come to fulfill the prophetic word to Paul through Ananias of Damascus that he would be sent to the Gentiles, 'to turn them from darkness to light, and from the power of Satan to God' (26:18). Paul used the year in Antioch to grow in his experience of ministering cross-culturally to Gentiles and to mature his theological reflection about what would be involved in his future career. I like to fantasize that Paul's time in Antioch would have been comparable to a year in a good School of World Mission!

The World's First "Christians"

....

> 11:26. ...And the disciples were first called Christians in
> Antioch.

....

Previous to this, Christians had been called believers, disciples, followers of the Way, or brothers and sisters. It is only when large numbers of Gentiles accepted Christ that the label "Christians" was put on them. From where did the name derive? It is used only twice more in Scripture: once by King Agrippa to Paul (see 26:28) and the other time by Peter when he referred to people suffering because of the name (see 1 Pet. 4:16). I agree with Simon Kistemaker who says, "We are inclined to think that the enemies of the faith ascribed this name to the Christians."[12]

It is not uncommon that a label, coined by outsiders sometimes in derision, becomes a permanent designation. Such a thing was true of Methodists and Quakers, to name just two examples. We are now so accustomed to being called "Christians," and proud of it, it seems strange that people would first use it to poke fun at born-again Gentiles.

A Prophetic Word to Share with the Poor

....

> 11:27. And in these days prophets came from Jerusalem
> to Antioch. 28. Then one of them, named Agabus, stood
> up and showed by the Spirit that there was going to
> be a great famine throughout all the world, which also
> happened in the days of Claudius Caesar. 29. Then the
> disciples, each according to his ability, determined to
> send relief to the brethren dwelling in Judea. 30. This

> they also did, and sent it to the elders by the
> hands of Barnabas and Saul.

....

This is the first time prophets and the gift of prophecy is mentioned in Acts. Many other aspects of power ministry have been introduced, but now we see the Holy Spirit speaking specific words to the church by recognized prophets. Not that prophecy was unexpected. On the Day of Pentecost, Peter had announced that Joel's prophecy was now being fulfilled, part of which was, **"I will pour out My Spirit in those days; and they shall prophesy"** (2:18). I would imagine prophecy was actually an ongoing part of the normal life of this early church, although Luke postpones spotlighting it until now.

The spiritual gift of prophecy is mentioned in Romans 12:6 and 1 Corinthians 12:10, and the *office* of prophet, which is second only to apostle, is mentioned in Ephesians 4:11. An office means that a person's particular spiritual gift has been recognized by the church and that the person is authorized to engage in open ministry centered around that gift. Agabus and the others had both the gift and the office because they were recognized prophets.

The office of prophet is gaining more stature in Christian churches around the world these days than it has in the recent past. The postdenominational churches particularly—representing the fastest-growing segment of global Christianity—are giving new prominence to prophets, but they are not doing so exclusively.

New Testament prophecy includes both foretelling and forthtelling. In Agabus's prophecy that **there was going to be a great famine throughout all the world** (Acts 11:28), we have an example of *foretelling*. That God wanted the believers in Antioch to help the poor in Jerusalem was *forthtelling*. This can be seen as an exemplary model for the blend of charismatic vitality and social action.

The believers in Antioch did what they were expected to do when they received an authentic prophetic word from God—they obeyed. They gave generously and sent the offering to Jerusalem with Barnabas and Paul.

Luke says they delivered the money **to the elders** (v. 30). Significantly, he doesn't say "apostles." This is an indication that the apostles were by then undoubtedly moving out from Jerusalem to spread the gospel, leaving the local church in the hands of those whom God had called and whom the apostles had trained for church leadership.

Reflection Questions

1. Reflect on the fact that in the time of the book of Acts, no church buildings, as such, were in existence. What implications might this have for our churches today?

2. Why might it not be considered unusual that the Hellenistic Jewish believers, when driven from Jerusalem, would not plant churches among Gentiles, including in predominantly Gentile cities?

3. The two-mission hypothesis suggested in this chapter is an important concept. Try to describe it in your own words. Explain how 8 to 10 years could have transpired between the two missions.

4. When the so-called CCM missionaries arrived in Antioch to plant Gentile churches, the only brothers and sisters in Christ would have been found in the Jewish quarter. Why would the missionaries prefer to live in other parts of the city far from fellow believers?

5. How about the name "Christian"? Why would the believers in Antioch, but not in Jerusalem, be called Christians? How do you like the name "Christian" today?

Notes

1. F. F. Bruce, *The Book of Acts* (Grand Rapids: William B. Eerdmans Publishing Co., 1954; revised edition, 1988), p. 224.
2. Simon J. Kistemaker, *Exposition of the Acts of the Apostles* (Grand Rapids: Baker Book House, 1990), p. 417.
3. W. J. Conybeare and J. S. Howson, *The Life and Epistles of St. Paul* (London: Longmans, Green and Co., 1875), p. 103.
4. I. Howard Marshall, *The Acts of the Apostles: An Introduction and Commentary* (Leicester, England: InterVarsity Press, 1980), p. 201.
5. Kistemaker, *Exposition of the Acts*, p. 418.
6. Bruce, *The Book of Acts*, p. 225.
7. Kistemaker, *Exposition of the Acts*, pp. 418-419.
8. R. C. H. Lenski, *The Interpretation of the Acts of the Apostles* (Minneapolis: Augsburg Publishing House, 1934), p. 450.
9. See Charles Van Engen, *God's Missionary People* (Grand Rapids: Baker Book House, 1991).
10. William Sanford LaSor, *Church Alive* (Ventura, CA: Regal Books, 1972), p. 167.
11. Stanley M. Horton, *The Book of Acts* (Springfield, MO: Gospel Publishing House, 1981), p. 140.
12. Kistemaker, *Exposition of the Acts*, p. 423.

The Power of Herod Versus the Power of Prayer

Luke is still in the process of making a transition from Peter as the central figure in the Acts of the Apostles to Paul. In the transition, he first tells of Paul's conversion, then how Peter evangelized the Gentiles in Cornelius's house, and then how Paul went to Antioch and began working with the first Gentile churches. Now we go back to Peter for the last time, except for his brief appearance a few years later at the Council of Jerusalem.

Actually, Acts 12 is a flashback. In Acts 11, Luke unfolded the story of church planting in Antioch, which took place over a period of 10 years or more. Acts 12 could have started off, "Meanwhile, in Jerusalem..." The whole chapter is like a parenthesis. Barnabas and Paul are on their way from Antioch to Jerusalem, carrying the offering the believers in Antioch had collected to help the poor. We would naturally wonder what had happened in Jerusalem. Were the elders surprised that the

Gentile believers in Antioch would send the Jews a gift? Were they pleased with the amount of money that came? Were many poor people actually helped? Did this social service give impetus to the growth of the Jerusalem church? These and many other questions like them did not seem to be of much interest to Luke. He gives us no information about the ministry of Barnabas and Saul in Jerusalem. When he finishes telling about Peter, Luke closes the parenthesis and simply says that Barnabas and Paul went back to Antioch.

The events Luke records in Acts 12 are not such historical milestones as were, for example, Paul's conversion, Peter's visit in Cornelius's house or Gentile churches being planted in Antioch. However, they are highly instructional for all of us who desire to be all that God wants us to be. The key lesson of the chapter is the power of prayer. I like the way Everett Harrison puts it: "The circumstances surrounding [Peter's] imprisonment are sketched in simple but dramatic fashion—the power of an earthly monarch pitted against the power of prayer to the Almighty."[1] We are looking at what many would call a power encounter.

Herod's Harassment

1. Now about that time Herod the king stretched out his hand to harass some from the church.

Who was **Herod the king**?

Herod was the surname of a family of rulers who served under the emperor of Rome. Three Herods are mentioned in the New Testament. Herod the Great is the one who had the babies killed soon after Jesus was born. Herod Antipas is the one who ordered the head of John the Baptist on a platter. This one is Herod Agrippa I, the grandson of Herod the Great. Then, to complete the picture, his son Herod Agrippa II is the one called King Agrippa before whom Paul defends himself in Acts 25. He was not known as "Herod" as his father was, but as "Agrippa."

Persecution did not seem to be a severe problem for the church in Jerusalem after the death of Stephen and after the Hellenistic Jewish believers were run out of town. An atmosphere of peaceful coexistence seemed to hold between the Jews who had believed that Jesus was Messiah and the other Jews. The major theological issue apparently had not surfaced among them, namely whether uncircumcised Gentiles could be saved without first becoming Jews. All Jerusalem males who had believed in Jesus up to that time had been circumcised. Even the Samaritans accepted the Pentateuch, which taught that circumcision was the norm, so their conversion seemed to be tolerated.

Years later, when we come to the Council of Jerusalem, it is surprising to some to find that many of the believers in Jerusalem, perhaps the majority, still maintained their theological ethnocentricity: **But some of the sect of the Pharisees who believed rose up, saying, "It is necessary to circumcise them, [the Gentile believers] and to command them to keep the law of Moses"** (15:5). This point of view satisfied the unbelieving Jews enough to shrug off those of their number who decided to become disciples of Jesus and, therefore, as Luke had said previously, **Then the churches throughout all Judea, Galilee, and Samaria had peace** (9:31).

But in the days of **Herod the king** something had changed. What was it?

Clearly, in my opinion, Peter's ministry in the house of Cornelius would have been the major event that had upset the status quo. Peter, a Hebrew Jew who some thought should have known better, had entered a Gentile house in Caesarea, had preached the gospel to a gathering of Gentiles there, and when they believed in Jesus Christ and were filled with the Holy Spirit, he baptized them without requiring circumcision. The apostles in Jerusalem were predictably upset when they first heard about this, but when Peter returned from his trip he succeeded in persuading them that it was valid for Gentiles to be saved and still remain Gentiles. This, however, was the beginning of serious trouble among other Jews in Jerusalem.

Meanwhile, the apostles had been training elders to take over the leadership of the Jerusalem church. When Barnabas and Paul carried the famine relief funds to Jerusalem, they delivered the money to the elders, not to the apostles. The apostles, who had come to agree with Peter that Gentile believers did not need to be circumcised, were by then out in a much wider itinerant ministry. At the time Herod stretched out his hand to harass some from the church (12:1), the apostles were no longer spending much of their time in Jerusalem. Everett Harrison suggests, "James, the brother of John, and Peter may have been the only members of the twelve in Jerusalem at the time."[2] They were the ones Herod put on his hit list.

James, the First Apostle to Die

···

2. Then he killed James the brother of John with the sword.

···

Although James, along with Peter and John, was one of Jesus' inner circle, he doesn't seem to have assumed a particularly prominent role in the leadership of the Jerusalem church. The James who later becomes a high-profile church leader is James the brother of Jesus Himself, not James the brother of John and the son of Zebedee.

Why, then, Herod singled out James is not altogether clear.

Although he was an apostle, he was perhaps a safer target than Peter, the recognized leader of the whole movement. As an apostle, James would have been identified with those who were tolerant of Gentile conversion. Although Luke does not furnish details, Herod undoubtedly would have worked with the Sanhedrin to indict James on some charge, perhaps one based on false accusations such as they did with Stephen, and then order his execution. James was killed **with the sword**, or beheaded, rather than being stoned as Stephen was. Richard Rackham concludes, "The charge, then, was one of disloyalty rather than of breaking the law."[3]

Peter Imprisoned to Please the Jews

> **3. And because he saw that it pleased the Jews, he proceeded further to seize Peter also. Now it was during the Days of Unleavened Bread. 4. So when he had apprehended him, he put him in prison, and delivered him to four squads of soldiers to keep him, intending to bring him before the people after Passover. 6. And when Herod was about to bring him out, that night Peter was sleeping, bound with two chains between two soldiers; and the guards before the door were keeping the prison.**

Killing James turned out to be a good political move. Herod **saw that it pleased the Jews.** He was on a roll. He held pleasing the Jews as a high value. Why? Because, strangely enough, according to Jewish law he had no right to be king over the Jews!

The family and descendants of Herod the Great were Jewish proselytes, Gentiles who had converted to Judaism. Herod the Great had married a Jewish woman, Mariamne, and wanted to be seen as a full Jew, so he went as far as to attempt to propagate a public lie through his court historian, Nicholas of Damascus, who, according to Joachim Jeremias, "spread it around that he was descended from the first Jews who returned from exile in Babylon."[4]

Although Herod the Great never actually succeeded in this deceit, the effort was an astute political move because, although proselytes were regarded as legitimate Jews in many things, they also had some implicit limitations. One of the most troublesome limitations was that, according to the official rabbinical interpretation of the law (Deut. 17:15) at that time, only a full-blooded Jew could be king. Jeremias says, "According to the law, Herod was an illegitimate usurper."[5]

Herod the Great's grandson, this Herod Agrippa I who had just killed James, was under the same stigma. At one point, a rabbi named Simon had succeeded in stirring up a public demonstration against him, saying that Herod had no right to go into the Temple because he was not a full-blooded Jew. Smarting from this, Herod had staged a showcase emotional appeal to win the sympathy of the general public.

According to custom, on a certain Jewish holiday the king should sit on a platform in the Temple and read the law to the people. Herod broke tradition and stood up instead of sitting down to grandstand his supposed humility and reverence for the law. Then Herod came to Deuteronomy 17:15: "You shall surely set a king over you whom the Lord your God chooses; one from among your brethren you shall set as a king over you; you may not set a foreigner over you, who is not your brother." When Herod read this, his voice cracked and he began weeping. Caught up in the emotion of the moment, the crowd of Jews cried out, "You are our brother! You are our brother!"[6]

As a good proselyte, Herod, of course, had been circumcised and kept the Jewish law. He offered sacrifices in the Temple and

observed the Passover. He had been accepted by his Jewish sub-
jects, but he always recognized that his position was precarious,
so whenever he could do something special to please the Jews
and relieve his identity crisis, he did it.

Now that Gentile circumcision had become an issue, killing
the apostle James was one way he could try to please the Jews. It
seemed to work so well that he decided he would up the ante and
attempt the same with Peter.

Doesn't murder seem to be a drastic extreme to secure a higher rating in political opinion polls? To many it might, but not to
the family of Herod. The demonic influence, especially the spirit of death, appeared to be extraordinarily strong through their
bloodline. The patriarch, Herod the Great, killed all the male
children under two years of age to try to eliminate the baby Jesus.
When he discovered that a group of rabbis had questioned
whether he should be king on the basis of what we have seen in
Deuteronomy 17:15, he had the rabbis arrested and executed
simply because their teaching did not please him. His son, Herod
Antipas, ordered John the Baptist's head cut off and he proudly
displayed it in front of his guests. For this current Herod, killing
James and Peter, who were now regarded by some Jews as troublemakers, would have been a relatively small thing to him as
long as it had good political results.

Demonic Principalities at Work

Jesus said, "The thief does not come except to steal, and to kill,
and to destroy" (John 10:10). I would not doubt that the actions
of these wicked Herods can be interpreted as more than ruthless
politics. Obviously, spiritual forces of darkness are strongly at
work here, desiring to keep the kingdom of God from spreading
throughout the world. It would be a severe setback for the bud-
ding Christian movement to lose its top leader and another apos-

tle at this point. But even more devastating for subsequent world evangelization would be enforcing the doctrine that all people, whoever they might be, need to be circumcised and become Jews to be saved.

Herod may or may not have understood this. But the forces of Satan, possibly headed up by the spirit of death, would certainly have understood, and they were using their wicked power to attempt to make it happen. That is why, under the surface, a power encounter between the forces of darkness and the forces of light is shaping up.

Herod decided to arrest Peter **during the Days of Unleavened Bread** (Acts 12:3). Astute as he was, Herod may have chosen the Passover because Jews from all over would be visiting Jerusalem at that time, and obviously, more Jews would be able to witness what he was doing. The public festivities would also have allowed the word to get around more easily that Peter was being held for trial until after the Passover. At that time the execution would take place, and little now could keep it from happening.

To avoid any possibility of his plans going awry, Herod took extraordinary security measures at the Jerusalem prison. He assigned **four squads of soldiers to keep him** (12:4). That would mean four soldiers at a time on six-hour shifts. Peter was **bound with two chains between two soldiers** (12:6), one soldier being chained to each of Peter's arms, and **the guards before the door were keeping the prison** (12:6). Maximum security!

Why would Herod take such unusual measures? Experience! Peter had been in the Jerusalem jail twice previously. The first time was with John for only one night, awaiting trial before the Sanhedrin the next day (see 4:3). The second time was with all of the apostles, and an angel had arrived during the night to free them without the guards outside knowing what had happened (see 5:17-23). This time Herod would not only post guards outside, but inside as well, chaining them to Peter so that not even an angel could free him.

Prayer Can Save Lives

> **12:5.** Peter was therefore kept in prison, but constant prayer was offered to God for him by the church.

This Scripture verse is fairly well known among biblical Christians, but it is not well applied in our Christian communities today. I believe it is the key verse in understanding Acts 12. The lesson is obvious: A cause-and-effect relationship was achieved between the prayer of the believers and Peter's release from prison. James was killed, and nothing is said about such a prayer meeting for him. Luke's silence does not mean, of course, that similar prayer for James *could* not have been offered. But whatever the case, we do know **that constant prayer was offered to God** on behalf of Peter and that the prayer was answered. Prayer was important enough to save Peter's life.

The phrase **constant prayer** is worth looking at for a moment. Other versions translate it as "earnestly praying" or "praying strenuously" or "praying unremittingly." This Greek word *ektenos* evidently is used to indicate a higher intensity of prayer than ordinary prayer. Luke uses it in another place to describe the intensity of Jesus' prayer in Gethsemane. There, Luke tells us that Jesus withdrew from the disciples "and He knelt down and prayed" (Luke 22:41). After a time an angel came and strengthened Him supernaturally. Following the angel's visit, Jesus went back to prayer and "He prayed more *earnestly* [*ektenos*]" (v. 44). This time when Jesus didn't pray in an ordinary way, but specifically prayed *earnestly*, "His sweat became like great drops of blood falling down to the ground" (v. 44). We recognize this as one of the most intense prayer times recorded in Scripture, but a similar level of prayer **was offered to God** (Acts 12:5) for Peter in Mary's house.

I personally became involved in the great worldwide prayer movement in 1987. Since then, I have associated a great deal with those who have been called to a special ministry of prayer in our time, those who have the spiritual gift of intercession. I am not among those who have the gift of intercession, but I have been with groups of intercessors, from time to time, when the intensity of prayer rises to a level roughly equivalent to Gethsemane. Those of us who have only average levels of spiritual sensitivity can often feel the spiritual power surging through such a group. The Holy Spirit comes in an unusual way, and time seems to stand still. It is a season of precious intimacy with the Father, and it brings a high degree of assurance that these prayers are being heard and acted upon in the heavenlies. A qualitative difference seems to occur between such **constant prayer** (*ektenos*) and the kind of prayer most of us are used to day in and day out.

The Gift of Intercession

Although any Christian can be caught up in such an intense level of prayer, and many could testify to that having happened on certain occasions, those who have the gift of intercession experience it more frequently. In my book *Your Spiritual Gifts Can Help Your Church Grow*, I define the gift of intercession as: "The special ability that God gives to certain members of the Body of Christ to pray for extended periods of time on a regular basis and see frequent and specific answers to their prayers, to a degree much greater than that which is expected of the average Christian."[7] After considerable research, my best estimate is that about 5 percent of the members of the Body of Christ have the gift of intercession.

By this I do not mean to imply that only a few Christians

should intercede for others. All of us in the 95 percent category have a role to be good pray-ers and intercessors. The difference is similar to all of us having a role to witness for Christ, but only a relatively few having been given the gift of evangelist. We can't all be a Billy Graham anymore than the whole body can be an eye. Nor do we all have the gift of intercession.

In my book *Prayer Shield* (Regal Books, 1992), I deal with the gift of intercession in considerable detail. My research has indicated that those who have the gift of intercession pray considerably longer than most. The minimum time period I found was one hour a day, but more normally those who have the gift pray between two and five hours each day. They enjoy prayer more, they see more frequent answers to their prayers, they hear from God more regularly and they pray more intensely.

Could it be that Mary, the mother of Mark, was one who had the gift of intercession? Although I couldn't prove it, I like to think she did. The prayer meeting for Peter took place in her house (see Acts 12:12), so Mary's house could have been one of the first houses of prayer. Her son, John Mark, was a close colleague of Peter's, and Peter's life was saved in Mary's house.

Does Prayer Change God's Plan?

Some, I know, have difficulty believing that, given the fact that a sovereign God has the whole world in His hands, Herod could have taken Peter's life just because some believers might have neglected to pray. Can we really say that a cause-and-effect relationship is effected between our human prayers and what God Almighty does? Although I fully accept the doctrine of the sovereignty of God, I also believe prayer does change things.

One thing prayer does *not* change is the nature of God. Nor is prayer some way we can manipulate God. This is what many of the defenders of God's sovereignty want to avoid, and I join them in this belief. However, the nature of God also includes involving human beings who have been reconciled to Him through Jesus Christ in His activities as members of His family. As God's will unfolds, God, in His sovereignty, decides not to predetermine all that will happen among human beings, but to make a certain number of things contingent upon human participation. For example, God is not willing that any lost soul should perish (see 2 Pet. 3:9), yet He entrusts preaching the gospel to human beings. If humans choose to disobey, lost people will not be saved. The same thing happens with prayer (see Jas. 4:2b). Richard Foster says, "We are working with God to determine the future. Certain things will happen in history if we pray rightly."[8]

If, implicitly or explicitly, we doubt whether anything will be changed by our prayers, we have just made a declaration of unbelief or lack of faith. Yet, faith is a key to seeing prayers answered. Jesus said, "If you have faith as a mustard seed, you will say to this mountain, 'Move from here to there,' and it will move; and nothing will be impossible for you" (Matt. 17:20). Jesus also said, "And all things, whatever you ask in prayer, *believing*, you will receive" (21:22, italics added).

In my book *Churches That Pray* (Regal Books, 1993), I call prayer that works "action prayer." Many churches in which prayer has been more in the rhetorical category are now moving into action prayer. The major element feeding the growing excitement about prayer is seeing answers to prayer. James says, "The effective, fervent prayer of a righteous man avails much" (Jas. 5:16). What does James mean by effective prayer? His illustration is of Elijah who prayed that it would not rain and it didn't rain for three years and a half, then he prayed again and it started raining. Considering these illustrations both from the Bible and from contemporary experience, Walter Wink can say with confidence, "History belongs to the intercessors."[9] It helps us believe all the more that prayer did, in fact, save Peter's life.

Back to Mary, the mother of Mark. Could this intercessor have been a personal prayer partner for Peter? Again, we have no direct evidence that she was, but it is a provocative possibility.

Personal Prayer Partners

Those who have the gift of intercession engage in four kinds of prayer ministries: general intercession, crisis intercession, personal intercession and warfare intercession. Some intercessors specialize in one, some in all four. Those to whom God gives a ministry of personal intercession pray a great deal for a particular leader or leaders. As I have frequently said, I believe intercession for Christian leaders is the most underutilized source of power in our churches today. I think much greater effectiveness in ministry would be released and considerably fewer pastors would fall into sin and leave the ministry if personal intercession were more widely recognized and used across the Body of Christ. I wrote my book *Prayer Shield* to help realize that goal.

My wife, Doris, and I have an inner circle of 21 personal intercessors and a wider circle of about 135. Whatever fruitfulness in ministry we enjoy, we attribute it primarily to the power of God released in our lives by the prayers of these faithful women and men. We have no hesitation in believing Peter's life was saved through the prayers of Mary and her friends, because we are convinced I would have been physically dead more than 10 years ago if it weren't for the **constant prayer** (Acts 12:5) (*ektenos*) of one of our intercessors, Cathy Schaller. The powers of darkness attempted to kill me by causing me to fall off a ladder 12 feet high, landing on the back of my head and neck on a cement floor on March 25, 1983. At exactly the same time, the Holy Spirit moved Cathy, who was attending a concert in a church 15 miles away, to enter into one of those times of intense prayer similar to Jesus' prayer in Gethsemane. After 20 minutes of travail she was released, knowing the victory had been won. I was discharged from the hospital having nothing more serious than severe bruises.

Doris and I had no doubt that my life had been in danger, because the Holy Spirit had spoken to Cathy during her intense prayer that the evil one had come to bring death and destruction. At the time, Cathy was still inexperienced in the ministry of intercession, but she had felt similar urges to pray for specific people on two other occasions during the preceding weeks. She did not yet know how to respond to those urges, however, and both of those people died! When my turn came, she responded and thank God she responded well!

Although we didn't know much about it at the time, Cathy Schaller had engaged in spiritual warfare. Satan and his forces of darkness lost that battle, because the power of God released through prayer was greater than any evil power he could muster in his attempt to kill me. A similar situation was taking place in Jerusalem here in Acts 12. Satan, in this case, was using a ruth-less king instead of a fall from a ladder to do away with a Christian leader. The believers in Mary's house went into intense spiritual warfare, described as **constant prayer**, and they also won the victory.

Prayer is the chief weapon of spiritual warfare. Many other weapons are available to be sure, but prayer stands at the top of the list. While Peter was in jail during Passover, a high-level power encounter was taking place in the invisible world. I would love to be able to interview Mary, the mother of Mark, to learn the details of what was happening in that prayer session. Having interviewed many contemporary intercessors who have entered similar situations of **constant prayer**, I can well imagine some of the things that might have been going on in the heavenlies.

Released by an Angel!

7. Now behold, an angel of the Lord stood by him, and a
light shone in the prison; and he struck Peter on the side
and raised him up, saying, "Arise quickly!" And his
chains fell off his hands. 8. Then the angel said to him,
"Gird yourself and tie on your sandals"; and so he did.
And he said to him, "Put on your garment and follow
me." 9. So he went out and followed him, and did not
know that what was done by the angel was real, but
thought he was seeing a vision. 10. When they were past
the first and the second guard posts, they came to the iron
gate that leads to the city, which opened to them of its
own accord; and they went out and went down one street,
and immediately the angel departed from him.

This is one of the clearest accounts we have of the visible and
tangible activity of an angel in the New Testament. As a part of
the spiritual drama of the power encounter that was taking place,
it would be well to go into some detail here. The title of this
chapter suggests that we are dealing with "the power of Herod
versus the power of prayer." How was the prayer of the Jerusalem
believers answered? As John Stott says, "Our understanding of
who this 'angel' was will depend largely on our presuppositions,
and in particular whether we believe in the existence of angels
and the possibility of the miraculous."[10] Certain ones who do not
believe in the miraculous theorize that some sort of internal conspiracy among the prison guard could have been taking place.
But knowing what Luke has already written about angels in the
Gospel of Luke, and earlier in Acts, we have no need to doubt
that he is describing the authentic activity of a literal angel.

A friend of mine recently complained that current literature on spiritual warfare has a good bit to say about demons, but not enough about angels. I agree. Another friend, Gary Kinnaman, a fellow member of the Spiritual Warfare Network, is helping remedy this with his new book, *Angels Dark and Light*. Others I know are beginning to shed more light on what we think of as the good angels, which happily outnumber the bad ones two to one, according to some calculations.

What Are Angels?

I like Gary Kinnaman's description of an angel. "Angels," he says, "are real. Angels are spiritual beings, godlike but not God. Nor are they human, or fleshy, although they may appear in human form. The precise 'substance' of their nature is unknown. They are immortal. They are not omnipresent—everywhere present at the same time—like God, but they are *immediately* present."[11] It was such a personal being who entered Peter's prison cell.

Why does God use angels? Why didn't the Holy Spirit Himself perform this miracle, as He apparently did when **the Spirit of the Lord caught Philip away** (8:39) from the Ethiopian eunuch and transported him bodily to Azotus, an equally notable miracle (see v. 40)? To me, the most satisfactory answer to this common question is not that God *has to* use angels at times to implement His will, but that He *wants to*. Sometimes He also uses human beings, and once in a while He uses demons, although against their will. On what basis God makes such choices we will probably never know in this life.

The Bible is clear from Genesis to Revelation, however, that God does use angels. Sometimes they are messengers, such as the one who told Mary she would give birth to the Messiah. Luke tells us that the angel's name was Gabriel (see Luke 1:26-38). At other times angels are delivery people, such as the one who took cake and water to Elijah (see 1 Kings 19:5-8). We see angels bringing answers to prayer, providing protection and ministering to God's people. "Are they [angels] not all ministering spirits sent forth to minister for those who will inherit salvation?" (Heb. 1:14).

Most readers find it amazing that Peter, in the midst of what would usually be an emotionally charged situation, was peacefully sleeping in the prison between the two Roman guards. We might expect that he would be praying or worshiping, as Paul and Silas would do later in the prison in Philippi, but he was only sleeping. Then the angel appears.

What does an angel really look like? Gary Kinnaman surveyed many people who had personally seen angels, in preparation for writing his book *Angels Dark and Light*. He reports "uncanny similarities" in the descriptions he received. "They are almost always very tall, usually around ten feet. They are bright, glowing white, often with a slight bluish tint. Their faces are indescribable, so their gender is unrecognizable. They are usually dressed in a full-length robe and frequently girded with a belt or sash of gold."[12] Most of those who have seen angels would know what Luke was talking about when he says **a light shone in the prison** (Acts 12:7).

Peter's release at the hands of the angel was so incredible that he himself didn't really believe it was happening. Removing the shackles with which he was chained to the guards without their knowing it (on a six-hour shift, professional military guards do not sleep), passing the two high-security guard stations outside, seeing the prison gate open as if it were on remote control, and finding himself in the streets of the city all alone was more than even an apostle of Jesus could assimilate quickly.

....

11. And when Peter had come to himself, he said, "Now I know for certain that the Lord has sent His angel, and has

> delivered me from the hand of Herod and from all
> the expectation of the Jewish people."

How long it would have taken Peter to come to himself is left to our imagination. He first expected to wake up from a dream while still in prison, but when he realized he had actually escaped from prison, he gave glory to God for the miracle. He soon headed directly for Mary's house where the all-night prayer meeting was still in progress.

> 12. So, when he had considered this, he came to the house
> of Mary, the mother of John whose surname was Mark,
> where many were gathered together praying.

Prayer and Spiritual Warfare

Prayer saved Peter's life. From the information Luke has provided for us, it was not so much Peter's personal prayers that saved his life as it was the prayers of other members of the Body of Christ, the intercessors. By this I do not mean to discredit Peter's personal prayer life or his spirituality in the least. But in this particular incident, Luke emphasizes not the prayers of the apostle, but that **constant prayer was offered to God for him by the church** (12:5).

This is similar to Joshua's famous victory over the Amalekites in Rephidim. The battle in Rephidim was won by God's power released through intercession. But the intercession that day was not Joshua's. He was fighting, not praying. It was Moses' intercession, aided by Aaron and Hur, that moved the hand of God and gave Joshua the victory (see Exod. 17:8-14). I think this is an excellent framework in which to understand the enormous spiritual power that can be released on behalf of Christian leaders, such as Joshua and Peter, through personal prayer partners. Not that intercession should ever be seen as a substitute for the leader's own prayer life, but we know from Scripture that it pleases God to respond to the prayers of intercessors and to release miraculous power that otherwise might have remained dormant. Details of how this is happening today can be found in my book *Prayer Shield.*

We should not lose sight of the magnitude of this power encounter. Whenever the human political authority over a population is involved, such as King Herod was, we can suspect that the spiritual battle is on the strategic or cosmic level (see Isa. 24:21 and Eph. 2:2). This power encounter was more than casting out a demon on the ground level or dealing with sorcery on the occult level. It undoubtedly involved the principalities and powers Paul writes about in Ephesians 6:12.

Peter's power encounter was similar to the spiritual battle in the heavenlies we are allowed to glimpse briefly as a result of the prayers of Daniel the prophet. Daniel prayed that (1) God would forgive Israel for the terrible sins they had committed against Him, and that (2) the Babylonian captivity of the Jews would end. God answered Daniel's prayer immediately by sending an angel to him, much as an angel was sent to Peter in prison. But in Daniel's case, it took the angel 21 days to arrive, because he was delayed by the Prince of Persia and needed the help of a stronger angel, Michael, to finally get through (see Dan. 10:1-14).

My point is that in both these cases we see human prayers answered by God through releasing powerful angels to implement His will. It is not always easy, either in the travail of human intercessors or in the invisible spiritual realm, because simultaneously the forces of darkness are using whatever means they have at their disposal to prevent the ministry of good angels. In Daniel's case, the forces of darkness were able to cause some delay. This is what we call spiritual warfare, and the intensity of the battle rises the higher we move through human structures that have authority over the well-being of entire human populations.

When the spiritual warfare involved rulers such as King Cyrus of Persia or King Herod Agrippa I of Judea, we can be sure it was extremely intense. Prayer was the key to victory both times: Daniel's solitary prayer and fasting for 21 days and the intercessors in Mary's house representing the church, or the Body of Christ, in Jerusalem. Daniel didn't know the battle had been going on in the heavenlies until the angel finally arrived. And the intercessors in Mary's house certainly didn't know because they could hardly believe it when Peter actually showed up.

Guardian Angels?

12:13. And as Peter knocked at the door of the gate, a girl named Rhoda came to answer. 14. When she recognized Peter's voice, because of her gladness she did not open the gate, but ran in and announced that Peter stood before the gate. 15. But they said to her, "You are beside yourself!" Yet she kept insisting that it was so. So they said, "It is his angel."

Predictably, the immediate aftermath of the miracle of Peter's release is causing no small amount of confusion. At first, the people in Mary's house thought Rhoda must have been kidding when she said Peter was there, and then they concluded, **"It is his angel."**

Why would the prayer participants have said this? Are such things as guardian angels in existence? Do people have their own personal angels assigned to accompany them? Do people's angels resemble those they serve?

The idea that people, especially children, have guardian angels is so prevalent that many assume it is something explicitly taught in the Bible. But such is not the case. The Bible teaches that such things as angels do exist and that, among other things, they do guard people, but we don't have any clear teaching that God does assign individual angels to guard every person on a one-to-one relationship. The Jerusalem believers exclaiming **"It is his angel"** is about as close as any biblical passage comes. And notice that this is just reporting a human opinion—an opinion, incidentally, of the same people who had just been wrong when they said to Rhoda, **"You are beside yourself!"** All we do know from this is that the concept that Peter might have **his angel** was common then, as it is among many today.

---

16. Now Peter continued knocking; and when they opened the door and saw him, they were astonished. 17. But motioning to them with his hand to keep silent, he declared to them how the Lord had brought him out of the prison. And he said, "Go tell these things to James and to the brethren." And he departed and went to another place.

When Peter instructs them to **"Go tell these things to James,"** he means James the brother of Jesus who became the leader of the church in Jerusalem. This is the last we hear of Peter in Acts other than his appearance in Acts 15. We do not know for sure where he went afterward or any details of his activities other than the little we can surmise from his two Epistles, which were written much later. Some think he later ministered in Rome.

King Herod: A Double Loser
It is doubtful Herod had any idea whatsoever that he was a chief

combatant in a high-level, spiritual power encounter. It seems that demonic forces must have been controlling him, and their plan had been to use him to throw roadblocks into the pathway of the advance of the kingdom of God. To the extent possible, they would have kept the king ignorant of what they were doing. When Herod failed with Peter, the spirit world had little more use for him.

---

18. Then, as soon as it was day, there was no small stir among the soldiers about what had become of Peter.
19. But when Herod had searched for him and not found him, he examined the guards and commanded that they should be put to death....

By losing his chance to execute Peter, Herod lost big time. It is true that capital punishment was the norm for guards who let their prisoners escape in those days, but Herod could easily have waived it. He was in no lenient mood, however, because he had spread the word all over Jerusalem during the days of the Passover that the Jews would be invited to Peter's execution. Peter's escape was a public embarrassment and, therefore, the soldiers lost their lives. Herod had lost the spiritual power encounter and paid the price. However, God was not through with Herod. The worst was yet to come!

---

20. Now Herod had been very angry with the people of Tyre and Sidon,.... 21. So on a set day Herod, arrayed in royal apparel, sat on his throne and gave an oration to them. 22. And the people kept shouting, "The voice of a god and not of a man!" 23. Then immediately an angel of the Lord struck him, because he did not give glory to God. And he was eaten by worms and died.

Herod had fallen deeper and deeper into perversity. Satanic forces apparently had gained free reign in his life until they brought him to make the same mistake Lucifer made when he was originally thrown out of heaven. Lucifer said, "I will be like the Most High" (Isa. 14:14). Herod accepted the cry of the crowd, **"The voice of a god and not of a man!"** (Acts 12:22).

As a matter of fact, the crowd might well have been right. Herod might have been speaking with the voice of a god that had a small g—in other words, the voice of a demonic principality. This claim to supernatural power brought a tangible application of what Paul writes about in Romans: "God gave them up" (see Rom. 1:24). Herod had "served the creature rather than the Creator" (v. 25); God gave him up, and that was the end for him.

The Spirit of Death

The fact that Herod died a horrible death **eaten by worms** (Acts 12:23) might be an indication that it was the spirit world, perhaps led by the spirit of death, that actually killed him. **An angel of the Lord** (12:23) was also involved. It would take a Frank Peretti to imagine what might be happening in the spirit world at the time. I am no Frank Peretti, but I have my personal suspicions. When I earlier described the monstrous wickedness and thirst for blood that came through the generations of Herods from Herod the Great, it appears that a spirit of death could have been passed from father to son. Some call such things "familiar spirits."

As reports come in from spiritual-mapping efforts being conducted in various parts of the world, the name "the spirit of death" seems to be emerging as one of the most powerful of all the ruling principalities of darkness. This may be connected with Paul's statement, "The last enemy that will be destroyed is death" (1 Cor. 15:26).

In Resistencia, Argentina, one of the first monitored and measured experiments in citywide spiritual mapping and strategic-level spiritual warfare focused on evangelism. It turned out that the most powerful of several spiritual principalities over the city was this very spirit of death. In Resistencia, the spirit of death also had a proper name, "San La Muerte," Spanish for "St. Death." People fervently worshiped and served this spirit because he had promised them a good death if they did so. A high priestess directed the cult that boasted 13 shrines scattered throughout the city. Many people had images of San La Muerte carved from human bone and surgically implanted under their skin so that San La Muerte would be with them always and at the end of their lives give them a good death.

These powers over the city of Resistencia had succeeded in keeping the gospel from spreading. The evangelical churches in Resistencia were weak, divided and had been plateaued for more than 10 years. The three-year experiment was conducted under Harvest Evangelism, directed by my friend Ed Silvoso. My wife, Doris, and Cindy Jacobs helped design and manage the strategic-level spiritual warfare phase of the project. The three years of ministry followed the guidelines found in Ed Silvoso's powerful book *That None Should Perish* (Regal Books, 1994). It was to culminate in a massive 11-day evangelistic crusade geared to reap the harvest God had been ripening over the months.

When Doris and Cindy arrived in Argentina for the evangelistic crusade, they were met with some grisly news. One week previously, the high priestess of the cult of San La Muerte had been smoking in bed. Her bed caught fire and the flames consumed three things: the mattress, the woman and her statue of San La Muerte 10 feet away. Nothing else was burned! Satan's perverse irony was to promise her a good death and then finish her off in a most gruesome way.

Our best assessment of the situation in Resistencia was that in all probability the high priestess's principal assignment from the devil at the time had been to prevent the evangelistic crusade from taking place. When she failed, the spirit world turned against her and killed her by fire. In Herod's case it was by worms. Either way, the fruit of the spirit of death is horrendous.

The battle lines had been set: The power of Herod versus the power of prayer. Because Christians were faithful in what some call "warfare prayer," the enemy was decisively defeated.

12:24. But the word of God grew and multiplied.

When the demonic obstacles are cleared away, the church can grow. Unbelievers are no longer blinded by the god of this age, and they now can hear and respond to the gospel. Luke gives us an upbeat account of what a power encounter can do for evangelism.

When I reported the details of the Argentina experiment in my book *Warfare Prayer*, I said, "The evangelical population of Resistencia virtually doubled in the calendar year of 1990."[13] By the end of the two subsequent years, the increase had gone from 100 percent to 500 percent! In Resistencia also **the word of God grew and multiplied.**

I like the way John Stott sums up Acts 12: "The chapter opens with James dead, Peter in prison, and Herod triumphing; it closes with Herod dead, Peter free, and the word of God triumphing."[14]

Reflection Questions

1. It is confusing to see the name "Herod" used for several people. Clear up some of this confusion by reviewing and identifying those who are named Herod.   *p. 114*

2. Why would Herod select the time of the Jewish Passover to carry out his plans to execute Peter? *P-120*
3. Reread the definition of the spiritual gift of intercession. What people have you known, or known of, who might have had this gift? *P-122*
4. To what extent could you agree with Richard Foster that, "Certain things will happen in history if we pray rightly"? Why? *P-124*
5. In this chapter we have explicit references to the real-life activity of angels. Have you ever had an experience that could be explained as a work of angels? Do you know anyone today who has? *P-132*

Notes

1. Everett F. Harrison, *Acts: The Expanding Church* (Chicago: Moody Press, 1975), p. 189.
2. Ibid., pp. 189-190.
3. Richard Belward Rackham, *The Acts of the Apostles* (London: Methuen & Co., Ltd., 1901), p. 176.
4. Joachim Jeremias, *Jerusalem in the Time of Jesus* (Philadelphia: Fortress Press, 1969), p. 331.
5. Ibid., p. 332.
6. Ibid., p. 333.
7. C. Peter Wagner, *Your Spiritual Gifts Can Help Your Church Grow* (Ventura, CA: Regal Books, 1979; revised edition, 1994), p. 68.
8. Richard J. Foster, *Celebration of Discipline* (San Francisco: HarperSanFrancisco, 1988), p. 35.
9. Walter Wink, *Engaging the Powers* (Minneapolis: Fortress Press, 1992), p. 299.
10. John Stott, *The Spirit, the Church and the World: The Message of Acts* (Downers Grove, IL: InterVarsity Press, 1990), p. 209.

11. Gary Kinnaman, *Angels Dark and Light* (Ann Arbor: Servant Publications, 1994), p. 20.

12. Ibid., p. 52.

13. C. Peter Wagner, *Warfare Prayer* (Ventura, CA: Regal Books, 1992), p. 33.

14. Stott, *The Spirit, the Church and the World*, p. 213.

Onward
to the Nations

Till this point, cross-cultural missions to the Gentiles have been incidental in Luke's writings. Now Luke turns his full attention to systematic, evangelistic missionary outreach to the Gentile world of the first century, and by extension, to all peoples of the world ever since. The motto of the A.D. 2000 and Beyond Movement, the great catalyst for world evangelization of the 1990s, is: *A church for every people and the gospel for every person by the year 2000.* The theme of the rest of Acts is how the gospel can be firmly planted in every unreached people group of the world.

By way of review, this is not the first time Luke mentions Gentile evangelism in Acts. Peter blazed the trail when he evangelized the Gentiles in the house of Cornelius in Caesarea. This occurred in about the year A.D. 40, and Luke describes the event in Acts 10. The second incident was the ministry of the Cyprus and Cyrene Mission (CCM) in Antioch where Gentile churches were first planted. This occurred in about the year A.D. 45, and Luke tells about it in Acts 11. Now we come to the ministry of Paul around the year A.D. 47.

Extending the Mission

....

12:25. And Barnabas and Saul returned from Jerusalem when they had fulfilled their ministry, and they also took with them John whose surname was Mark.

....

In the last chapter, I pointed out that Acts 12 was like a paren-thesis. It began with Barnabas and Paul taking relief funds from Antioch to Jerusalem, but the rest of the chapter tells of Peter's power encounter with King Herod. The end of the chapter closes the parentheses, and the last verse actually belongs here with Acts 13. It opens with Barnabas and Paul returning to Antioch and young John Mark joining them. Mark's mother's house was the house of prayer in Jerusalem and she, I suspect, was a personal intercessor for Peter. Who knows if Mary might have also been called to be a special intercessor for Barnabas and Paul now that her son had joined their ministry team?

....

13:1. Now in the church that was at Antioch there were certain prophets and teachers: Barnabas, Simeon who was called Niger, Lucius of Cyrene, Manaen who had been brought up with Herod the tetrarch, and Saul.

....

This passage of Scripture is so important for Christian mis-sions that it becomes a topic of conversation in missiological cir-cles just about as frequently as any other part of the Bible. Through the years, I have identified three questionable conclusions that some have drawn from this verse and the surrounding passage. The three conclusions I believe need to be reexamined are:

- Acts 13 marks the beginning of cross-cultural missions to the Gentiles.
- The church at Antioch was an ethnically mixed local congregation.
- The Antioch church was the missionary-sending agency under which Barnabas and Paul were sent out and to which they were accountable.

Let me explain.

Cross-cultural missions to the Gentiles did not begin here, but in Acts 11 when the missionaries from Cyprus and Cyrene went to Antioch with the express purpose of planting churches among the Gentiles in the Gentile quarters of the city. Previously, Hellenistic Jewish missionaries had gone to Antioch to plant Messianic Jewish churches in the Jewish quarter. I explained this in considerable detail in chapter 3.

The Church at Antioch

It is easy to interpret the list of Barnabas, Simeon Niger, Lucius, Manaen and Saul as a selection of typical members of the church at Antioch. It is also easy to visualize the church at Antioch as if it were a fairly large congregation of believers that met together on Sunday mornings for worship, heard the same sermon and developed a church program to meet the needs of its people. This is because the natural tendency is to relate "church" to the kind of church most of us attend from week to week.

This was far from the situation in Antioch. To review what we discussed in chapter 3, Antioch was a huge cosmopolitan city of 500,000. The Jews lived in a Jewish ghetto of 25,000, and those among them who had believed in Jesus and had become

Messianic Jews had been meeting with each other in homes for some 10 years before any Gentile churches were planted at all. They had no central location where they would all meet together on a regular basis, for as Jews they attended their own synagogues on the Sabbath. They abstained from pork, kept the Passover, married their children to other Jews, circumcised their male offspring and held the belief, perhaps with differing degrees of conviction, that Gentiles needed to be circumcised and become Jews in order to know God properly. They would not allow Gentiles either in their synagogues or in their homes. To eat in a Gentile home was unthinkable to them. They were notably ethnocentric, to put it mildly.

The CCM missionaries (as I have called them) evangelized the 475,000 Gentiles in various parts of the city neighborhood by neighborhood. Again, they had no central church building, but rather, house churches. Antioch was a multicultural and multilinguistic city. In Antioch, as in cities throughout human history, residents who shared the same language, customs and marriage market tended to live in geographical proximity. How do I know this? I admit it is based on an assumption—Antioch was a fairly normal city that followed predictable patterns of urban sociology and anthropology.

The Antioch churches were all house churches or neighborhood churches. How many of the Antioch Gentile people groups such as those of the Syrians, Greeks, Romans or any number of others had networks of house churches growing among them we do not know. But whatever the number, the rule among them, with very few exceptions, if any, would be that the people who met regularly in any of the neighborhood house churches would have lived near each other and been from the same people group. On occasion, larger groups of them might have met together for specific purposes. Everett Harrison says, "It is likely that several groups met in homes throughout [Antioch], though we should not rule out the possibility that some public meetings for evangelistic purposes were held in halls."[1]

Keeping this picture in mind, Luke's phrase **the church that was at Antioch** (13:1) would include substantial numbers of neighborhood house churches, but not one master organization. Missiologist Dean S. Gilliland puts it this way: "The most important feature of the church was the multitude of small units, each of which met together, working out its new life in sharing blessings and working through problems. It is error to think even of Paul's urban churches as large single congregations."[2]

Antioch's Prophets and Teachers

Church offices are beginning to appear. In the Jerusalem church we have seen that the leaders first were the *apostles*, who then became mostly itinerant, and later *elders* who presumably were the residents of Jerusalem and to whom Barnabas and Paul delivered the offering for the poor donated by the church at Antioch. The churches had *prophets* as well, because Luke mentions, **In these days prophets came from Jerusalem to Antioch** (Acts 11:27).

In Antioch, five people are listed as **prophets and teachers** (13:1). This implies the office of prophet and the office of teacher. A church office signifies that the church has recognized a particular spiritual gift the Holy Spirit has given to a person, and has authorized that person to minister with this gift in the church. Thus it can be assumed that these five had been given the spiritual gifts of prophecy and teaching. What is the difference? Here are the definitions found in my book *Your Spiritual Gifts Can Help Your Church Grow*:

Prophecy. The gift of prophecy is the special ability

that God gives to certain members of the Body of Christ to receive and communicate an immediate message of God to His people through a divinely anointed utterance.

Teaching. The gift of teaching is the special ability that God gives to certain members of the Body of Christ to communicate information relevant to the health and ministry of the Body and its members in such a way that others will learn.[3]

In general, the prophets received new information from God while the teachers explained what was revealed to the church. It is not known which of the five would have been prophets and which would have been teachers, or which might have been operating in both gifts simultaneously. William Ramsay thinks a certain Greek construction might indicate that Barnabas, Simeon and Lucius were prophets, while Manaen and Paul were teachers[4] but few other biblical scholars see it that way. My research on spiritual gifts shows that most Christians, especially leaders, have gift-mixes rather than solitary gifts, and that could well have been the case in Antioch.

If we read this passage rapidly, the fact might escape us that none of the five was a long-term resident of the city of Antioch. None ministered as an elder of one of the many house churches that were by then in full operation in Antioch, so the prophets and teachers (13:1) were not also called "elders." More than likely, they were what we would see today as the foreign missionaries who were helping to establish the national church. No information we are given would prevent us from concluding that the five were members of the CCM, the Cyprus and Cyrene Mission I described in detail in chapter 3. Let's consider the five men one at a time.

Barnabas was a Hellenistic Jew born in Cyprus. He was one of the charter members of the Jerusalem church, and one of those who sold their property and donated the proceeds to the congregation (see 4:36,37). From that, it could well be taken that he was somewhat affluent. Being a Cyprian, Barnabas could easily have identified with the CCM missionaries who had gone from Cyprus to evangelize the Gentiles in Antioch (see 11:20). That might have been one reason the leaders of the church in Jerusalem would have chosen him as the one to go to Antioch when they received the news that Gentiles were becoming believers there and that Gentile churches were rapidly forming.

It is not beyond reason to suppose that Barnabas, who must have left Jerusalem when the persecution came after Stephen's death because he was one of the Hellenists, could have been among those said to have gone from Jerusalem to Cyprus (see 11:19). If so, he could have helped plant the first church among the Hellenistic Jews there, and that could have been one of the churches that supported the CCM. Barnabas, therefore, might have been a founder and a financial backer of the Cyprus and Cyrene Mission, which he would likely have joined as a field missionary when he arrived in Antioch.

Simeon was called Niger, the Latin word for black. Biblical scholars agree that he was probably from Africa, and he could have been from the North African nation of Cyrene. He also could have been one of the original CCM missionaries to Antioch.

Lucius is said to be from Cyrene and even more likely a charter member of the CCM. Both Simeon and Lucius would have been Hellenistic Jews who had believed in Jesus as their Messiah. Some think they might have been converted in Jerusalem and left after Stephen's death, but no one knows for sure.

Manaen is said to have been brought up with Herod the tetrarch (13:1), possibly as a foster brother. Herod the tetrarch, who ruled over Judea and Perea, was the one who had John the Baptist beheaded. He and Manaen would have grown up in the palace of Herod the Great, which was in Caesarea. Manaen would have been a Jew because, as we have seen, Herod the Great constantly attempted to mask the fact that he was a proselyte and pretended that he was a full-blooded Jew. He would not have invited a non-Jew into his family. Kistemaker describes Manaen as "an influential person of royal descent."[5]

Saul was, of course, from Tarsus, not from Antioch.

All five of the **prophets and teachers** were, according to my hypothesis, foreign missionaries who had gone to Antioch on assignment. Because they had been ministering among the networks of house churches in Antioch, Luke can accurately describe them as being **in the church that was at Antioch.** If, as I suspect, they had planted a truly indigenous church, they would have by then turned the leadership over to the believers who were long-term, permanent residents of Antioch and they would not have made the mistake many missionaries have made since of attempting to serve as elders of the national church. The five, perhaps along with others, functioned as what we call today a "parachurch organization"—the Cyprus and Cyrene Mission.

Pioneering New Fields

....

2. As they ministered to the Lord and fasted, the Holy Spirit said, "Now separate to Me Barnabas and Saul for the work to which I have called them."

....

As a missionary team, the CCM members often would have withdrawn from the church for their own meetings. Waiting before the Lord in worship and prayer would have been a common experience for them. In this case they were also fasting. F. F. Bruce says, "There are indications in the New Testament that Christians were specially sensitive to the Spirit's communication during fasting."[6] As prophets, they would already have become accustomed to receiving direct revelation from God, so they had no problem in recognizing the word of the Holy Spirit to them clearly enough to put it in quotes: **"Now separate to Me Barnabas and Saul for the work to which I have called them."** Here is one more case, added to many we have already seen, of verbal instructions from God so specific that when the Antioch leaders later might have asked why they were sending Barnabas and Paul away, the answer would have been, "Because God told us to."

Sodality Versus Modality

Keep in mind that Barnabas and Paul did not first become missionaries at this point. They were already missionaries, simply being reassigned. The process of hearing from God and reassigning the missionaries accordingly took place within what missiologists call the "sodality," or the CCM mission agency, not the "modality," or the Antioch church as such.

In 1974, missiologist Ralph D. Winter published a landmark essay called "The Two Structures of God's Redemptive Mission," laying the groundwork for subsequent modality-sodality theory.[7] In his essay, Winter established the fact that in biblical times, such as here in Antioch, the existing Jewish synagogue structure was largely adopted as the structure for local Christian churches, while the existing Jewish proselytizing bands were largely adopted as the model for missionary-sending organizations such as the CCM. The former he labels "modalities" and the latter "sodalities." For technical reasons, sodality seems to be a better term than parachurch because in the broader sense, the sodality is legitimately part of the "church."

Winter convincingly, then, shows that throughout history, the predominant structure for the extension of the kingdom of God into new mission frontiers has been the sodality, not the modality. Each has its essential place in the Kingdom, but for cross-cultural missions God seems to have favored the sodality. This is why I believe it is important to understand that in Antioch the Holy Spirit evidently spoke to the sodality (the CCM) instead of the modality (the Antioch church) to **"separate to Me Barnabas and Saul for the work to which I have called them"** (13:2).

Commissioning Workers

....

3. Then, having fasted and prayed, and laid hands on them, they sent them away. 4. So, being sent out by the Holy Spirit, they went down to Selucia,....

....

Fasting is again mentioned as a fairly routine spiritual discipline for the missionaries. Prayer and laying on of hands were an important part of the commissioning as well. Who laid on hands? As far as the text is concerned, the other three would have laid hands on Barnabas and Saul. Whether any others from either the sodality or the modality would have been invited to participate is a matter of conjecture. Most students of Acts think the church in general would have played some role. In all probability it did, but it should be seen as a secondary, not a primary, role.

Some scholars point out an interesting use of two Greek words for "to send" here. Obviously, the chief sending agent was the Holy Spirit, and the Greek verb in **So, being sent out by the Holy Spirit** is *pempo*, which is usually a more proactive kind of sending or dispatching. The "send" in **they sent them away** is from the Greek word *apoluo*, which frequently means releasing something that has its own, or another, source of energy. It could be said that "they released them." Certainly here we have a combination of the two kinds of sending and the spiritual power for missionary activity coming from the Holy Spirit.

East Cyprus and the Synagogues

---

4. So, being sent out by the Holy Spirit, they went down to Selucia, and from there they sailed to Cyprus. 5. And when they arrived in Salamis, they preached the word of God in the synagogues of the Jews. They also had John as their assistant.

Selucia is the seaport that serves Antioch. From Selucia, Barnabas and Paul went to Cyprus, an island about 60 miles away, which would take less than a day to cross. Cyprus is about 140 miles long from east to west, and it was Barnabas's home territory. The principal city to the east is Salamis and the principal city to the west is Paphos.

In Salamis, Barnabas and Paul **preached the word of God in the synagogues of the Jews.** This is about all we know for certain about their first stop on the missionary excursion. But it is important because it establishes a strategic pattern for most of Paul's subsequent evangelistic ministry. Whenever a city had a synagogue, Paul would begin his evangelistic work there. He apparently bypassed certain cities because they did not have a synagogue. Paul did this for several reasons.

First, Paul had a *theological reason.* The Abrahamic covenant has never been nullified. Paul later says, "For I am not ashamed of the gospel of Christ, for it is the power of God to salvation for everyone who believes, for the Jew first and also for the Greek" (Rom. 1:16). As things work out, the Jews as a people group eventually reject the gospel and the Gentiles are grafted in, but to the same roots coming from Abraham (see chap. 11).

Second, Paul had a *social reason*. The law of natural affinity would indicate that Paul would probably first seek out those of his own kith and kin. Wherever it might be in the Roman Empire, the Jewish community would be for Paul at most a moderate E-2 distance rather than the more radical E-3 distance.

Third, Paul had a *strategic reason*. Because Paul was called to be an apostle to the uncircumcision, his ultimate goal was to make disciples among Gentiles and to plant Gentile churches. The best place to start at that point in history, however, was the Jewish synagogue. As I have pointed out previously, three distinguishable groups of people were attached to most Jewish synagogues in the first century:

- Jews who could trace their ancestry to Abraham.
- Proselytes who were born Gentiles, but who chose to convert and to become Jews instead.
- God-fearers who were also born Gentiles, but who chose to maintain their Gentile identity while associating with the synagogue as best they could, so they could follow Jehovah God.

The God-fearers of the synagogue communities were by far the most receptive people to Paul's message as he traveled from place to place. Why this is true I will explain in detail when Barnabas and Paul arrive in **Antioch in Pisidia** (Acts 13:14) shortly. Meanwhile, we understand why they established such a pattern at the very beginning of their missionary journey.

They also had John as their assistant (13:5). This is John Mark, who may have been with them ever since they returned from Jerusalem to Antioch after taking the offering for the poor (see 12:25). Mark becomes important later when he and his cousin Barnabas precipitate a mission split.

West Cyprus and the Power Encounter

....

13:6. Now when they had gone through the island to
Paphos, they found a certain sorcerer, a false prophet,
a Jew whose name was Bar-Jesus, 7. who was with the
proconsul, Sergius Paulus, an intelligent man. This man
called for Barnabas and Saul and sought to hear the
word of God.
8. But Elymas the sorcerer (for so his name is translated)
withstood them, seeking to turn the proconsul away from
the faith. 9. Then Saul, who is also called Paul, filled with
the Holy Spirit, looked intently at him 10. and said, "O full
of all deceit and all fraud, you son of the devil, you enemy of
all righteousness, will you not cease perverting the straight
ways of the Lord?
11. And now, indeed, the hand of the Lord is upon you, and
you shall be blind, not seeing the sun for a time." And
immediately a dark mist fell on him, and he went around
seeking someone to lead him by the hand.

....

Paphos was the capital of Cyprus in those days. Whether a synagogue was located in Paphos we are not told, but we have no reason to conclude that one did not exist and that Paul did not visit
it first, simply because Luke doesn't mention it. Luke had something much more momentous to write about in West Cyprus.
Living in Paphos was **the proconsul, Sergius Paulus, an intelligent man.** With the Roman proconsul, in some sort of an established relationship, was **a certain sorcerer, a false prophet, a Jew
whose name was Bar-Jesus.**

Luke is setting the scenario for one of the major episodes of
spiritual warfare in the New Testament. John Stott remarks that
Luke "brings before his readers a dramatic power encounter, in
which the Holy Spirit overthrew the evil one, the apostle con-

founded the sorcerer, and the gospel triumphed over the occult."[8] Yale biblical scholar Susan Garrett puts it plainly: "The confrontation between Bar Jesus and Paul is also a confrontation between the Holy Spirit and the devil."[9]

What is a power encounter? A power encounter is a practical, visible demonstration that the power of God is greater than the power of the spirits worshiped or feared by the members of a given social group or by individuals. A prominent Old Testament example is seen when Elijah challenged the prophets of Baal on Mount Carmel. God visibly demonstrated His superior power by lighting the fire on the altar, and as a part of the aftermath the prophets of Baal were executed (see 1 Kings 18:20-40).

Strategic-Level Warfare?

Was the power encounter in West Cyprus an example of strategic-level spiritual warfare?

To review, the three levels of spiritual warfare most frequently dealt with are *ground-level spiritual warfare*, which deals with casting demons out of an individual; *occult-level spiritual warfare*, which deals with the demonic forces behind witchcraft, sorcery, Satanism and other forms of the occult; and *strategic-level spiritual warfare*, which deals with confronting the territorial spirits that may control a city, a people group or some other human social network.

No one would question that, in agreement with John Stott, this story is one of the gospel triumphing over the occult. But, could it possibly have reached higher than the occult level? This is a plausible question because of the relationship between the sorcerer and the highest-ranking political figure of the area, the Roman proconsul Sergius Paulus. Alliances between political leaders and the occult are extremely common today as well. They are not simply curiosities of history, as illustrated closer to home by the ongoing relationship Mrs. Ronald Reagan maintained with an astrologer to advise her in arranging the president's schedule.

Much about this story we do not know, such as the precise identity of the spiritual principality that was using Bar-Jesus as an instrument to keep Sergius Paulus in darkness. But whatever the identity, the angel of darkness assigned to Sergius Paulus was much more than a standard rank-and-file demon. To underline the scale of this conflict, Susan Garrett points out, "Bar Jesus is closely linked with the figure of Satan."[10]

Sergius Paulus was open to the gospel. He was an **intelligent man** who **called for Barnabas and Saul and sought to hear the word of God** (Acts 13:7). This potentially could have been a major key to open the whole region to the kingdom of God. The chief opponent was Bar-Jesus who **withstood them, seeking to turn the proconsul away from the faith** (v. 8). If Bar-Jesus failed, he would lose his job, because there would be no more need for a court magician. More ominously, he was in danger that his spiritual masters, whoever they might have been, would likely turn against him because he had failed them and their ruler, Satan. He would have had good reason to be terrified of the punishments imposed by the kingdom of darkness.

What was at stake?

The issue here was power; in this case not truth or morality. The lines were clearly drawn. In the visible world it was Paul versus Bar-Jesus. In the invisible world, as Susan Garrett says, "The human combatants Paul and Bar-Jesus in turn represent superhuman figures."[11] It was a clash of two kingdoms: the kingdom of God invading the kingdom of Satan. Because each side shared a common worldview that informed them of the interplay between the invisible world and the visible world, they well knew the rules of combat. The prize in the natural was the conversion of Sergius Paulus, but spiritually it could have been the opening of perhaps all of Cyprus to the gospel of Christ.

Paul was **filled with the Holy Spirit** (13:9) while his opponent, Bar-Jesus, was **"full of all deceit and all fraud,"** explicitly
a **"son of the devil"** (13:10).

Having the filling of the Holy Spirit, Paul was in intimate
contact with the Father. In a power encounter of this magnitude
it is essential to know for certain what the Father's will is at the
precise moment. Paul's words **"you shall be blind, not seeing the
sun for a time"** (13:11) should be taken as God's words spoken
through Paul. Paul himself might have been surprised at the
words coming out of his mouth. Many Christian leaders can tell
of occasions when they believed that what they were speaking
had not been premeditated, but rather, they were words that were
being given to them supernaturally.

God's power prevailed, and the sorcerer was blind for a period
of time. The event, of course, was public and the news would
have spread far and wide in a short time. Jesus Christ would be
seen by many to be the true Lord over Paphos and all of Cyprus.

Teaching by Word and Deed

**12. Then the proconsul believed, when he saw what had
been done, being astonished at the teaching of the Lord.**

It is interesting that the trigger point for the proconsul's conversion was not so much what he *heard* as what he *saw*. He was
astonished at the teaching of the Lord, indicating that the kind
of teaching Paul was doing was teaching both in word and in
deed. One of the shortcomings of some Western missionaries in
modern times has been their strong emphasis on the word and
little on the deed. Fortunately, today's missionary force is now
including many missionaries from the non-Western world. A

report that came back from people in the Himalayas recently said, "The Western missionaries brought us the knowledge of God, but the Third World missionaries are bringing us the power of God." The implication of the message was that the gospel is spreading much more rapidly now that visible demonstrations of God's power are accompanying the spoken message of the gospel.

More and more Western missionaries are now beginning to tune in to the kind of spiritual power demonstrated by the apostle Paul in West Cyprus. A deterrent in the past has been the failure of many of us to understand the awesome authority given to us by Jesus Christ through the Holy Spirit. Jesus said to His disciples, "Behold, I give you the authority...over all the power of the enemy" (Luke 10:19). Some believe this authority is over only the lower-ranking demons, but here in Cyprus we have seen that it was interpreted as power over Satan himself. Could we be bold enough to take what Jesus termed "all the power of the enemy" literally?

This is important for evangelism because, as Paul later wrote, the essential reason the glory of Christ does not penetrate to unbelievers is that "the god of this age has blinded [their minds]" (2 Cor. 4:4). This pitches the battle on its highest plain because the "god of this age" is the devil himself. Here in West Cyprus, Paul was learning how to use this authority to get the blinders imposed by Satan through Bar-Jesus off the eyes of Sergius Paulus. Susan Garrett asks how Paul could attempt to do such a thing, and then says, "The answer is that *Paul must be invested with authority that is greater than Satan's own* [emphasis hers]. In depicting Paul's successful unmasking and punishment of Bar Jesus, Luke is saying that Paul could do the work to which he had been called because he possessed authority over all the power of the Enemy (cf. Luke 10:19)."[12]

Some Mission Business

13:13. Now when Paul and his party set sail from Paphos,
they came to Perga in Pamphylia; and John, departing
from them, returned to Jerusalem.

Three significant changes take place in the affairs of the mission
at this point.

Paul's name changes. Up till the power encounter with Bar-Jesus,
Luke had been using the Jewish name, Saul. From this point on, he
uses the Roman name, Paul. This will further emphasize that Paul's
calling was that of a missionary to the uncircumcision.

The leadership changes. Luke, up till this point, has always said
Barnabas and Saul (v. 7). Now for the first time we read **Paul
and his party.** Paul is regarded from here on as the leader.

John Mark resigns from the mission. Why did John Mark turn
back? Depending on the biblical scholar you select, it could have
been because he was homesick, because he didn't feel they should
direct their ministry primarily at Gentiles, because he was afraid
to travel through the dangerous Taurus Mountains where they
were headed, or because his cousin, Barnabas, had taken a subor-
dinate place in the mission to Paul. Because every reason is an
educated guess, it might not be out of order if I add one more.

Mark's resignation could have been because he didn't feel
called to the kind of high-level spiritual warfare he had just witnessed in Paphos. As the challenge of strategic-level spiritual
warfare has been on the increase in the 1990s, it has become
clear that many good Christians and good Christian leaders do
not want to have anything to do with it. This is perfectly normal.
Gideon started with 32,000 men and, by God's direction, nar-
rowed his army down to 300. The 300 were where God wanted

them to be, and also the 31,700, who didn't go to the battle, were where God wanted them to be (see Judg. 6—7). If this pattern holds, it could well have been God's will that Mark be in Jerusalem rather than in south Galatia where they were heading. The fact that Paul didn't agree and later held it against Mark (see Acts 15:36-40) is incidental.

On to Turkey

> **13:14. But when they departed from Perga, they came to Antioch in Pisidia, and went into the synagogue on the Sabbath day and sat down.**

Paul and his entourage would have traveled about 150 miles by ship and landed in the port of Adalia (today Antalya) in what we now know as Turkey. They continued 12 miles inland to Perga in the province then known as Pamphylia. Perga was a Greek city featuring a large temple constructed to give honor to Artemis, one of the highest-ranking principalities in the Roman Empire, who had headquarters in Ephesus where she was also known as Diana of the Ephesians. Because some of the most instructive episodes of spiritual warfare in the ministry of Paul take place in Ephesus, we will postpone discussing Diana until we come to Acts 19.

Meanwhile, why did **Paul and his party** (v. 13) not stop to preach and plant a church in Perga? Although we are not specifically told, a compelling enough reason would be that possibly Perga had no synagogue. Later Paul passes through Amphipolis and Apollonia, presumably for the same reason (see 17:1). In both cases, the synagogue is specifically mentioned as a reason why they did stop where they did: **Antioch in Pisidia** here in this text (13:14) and **Thessalonica** in 17:1.

We should also take note that although the temple to Artemis was located in Perga and the most elementary spiritual mapping would presumably show she was the territorial spirit ruling over the city, just knowing this is not reason enough for engaging in strategic-level spiritual warfare. Paul was an accomplished spiritual warrior, but not trigger happy. Obviously, God's will and His timing were different in Perga than in Paphos where God did direct Paul to engage in a high-level power encounter. It is dangerous to the extreme to take on high-ranking demonic forces without the clear leading of the Lord and the filling of the Holy Spirit such as Paul had in West Cyprus.

Later, as we shall see, Paul did stop and preach in Perga (see 14:25). Evidently the situation there had changed by then.

Antioch in Pisidia

They came to Antioch in Pisidia (13:14). This 100-mile trip on foot through rugged mountains was not easy. Among other things, it was known as a region infested with bandits who preyed on travelers. Some think that when Paul later said he had been "in perils of robbers" (2 Cor. 11:26), he could well have been reflecting on this particular trip. The name "Antioch" often causes confusion because it is the same name as the city of Antioch in Syria where Paul and Barnabas started this journey. Many cities were named Antioch in those days because a king named Antiochus had tried to immortalize himself by putting his name on as many cities as possible.

Why did Paul and Barnabas target **Antioch in Pisidia?** One reason could be that it was in Paul's home territory just as Cyprus had been Barnabas's home territory. Further, it was a leading city of the region and on a major trade route. But I think the most important determining factor was that a synagogue of the Jews was located in **Antioch in Pisidia.** Many receptive God-fearers were active in that synagogue.

It is also well to keep in mind that Antioch is in the region of Galatia. Soon after Paul ministered there, he wrote his first epistle to the churches, the Epistle to the Galatians. What we are about to see here has great missiological significance for the future, and this is a reason I will later include a whole chapter on the book of Galatians (chapter 7). What happens here in Antioch sets a pattern that all who engage in cross-cultural evangelism and missions need to understand as thoroughly as possible.

Paul and the others **went into the synagogue on the Sabbath day and sat down** (13:14). Then:

> **15. And after the reading of the Law and the Prophets, the rulers of the synagogue sent to them, saying, "Men and brethren, if you have any word of exhortation for the people, say on."**

It is good to remind ourselves that although Paul was an apostle of Jesus Christ, he was still a Jew. Furthermore, Paul was a rabbi of some prestige among first-century Jews. Because his family lived in Tarsus, about 250 miles to the east on the same trade route, Paul and his relatives would likely have been known or have had personal friends in the Jewish quarter of **Antioch in Pisidia**. It is not everyone who could claim to be a disciple of the famous rabbi Gamaliel. For these reasons, Paul was invited to speak.

The sermon Paul preached, which is Paul's first recorded sermon, is extremely significant. It is a long sermon as far as biblical sermons go. If measured by the number of Bible verses Luke dedicates to it, only two sermons in Acts are longer: Stephen's sermon to the Sanhedrin in Acts 7 (52 verses), and Peter's sermon on the Day of Pentecost in Acts 2 (36 verses). Paul's sermon includes 26 verses. As was the case with the other two sermons,

I will not reproduce it as a whole here, but simply highlight the most significant features.

Paul's First Recorded Sermon

....

13:16. Then Paul stood up, and motioning with his hand said, "Men of Israel, and you who fear God, listen:"

....

Paul addresses two audiences simultaneously: (1) **"Men of Israel."** These are Jews, including proselytes, who keep the law, circumcise their male children and strictly maintain a kosher kitchen. (2) **"You who fear God."** These are uncircumcised Gentiles who are attracted to the synagogue community and to God, but who have remained Gentiles and who have not promised to keep the whole law. They are not members of the synagogue per se.

By now, Paul has learned that *as far as his mission to plant Gentile churches as an apostle of the uncircumcision is concerned*, his primary audience in the synagogue community is the God-fearers. The ethnic Jews are also important, and some of them get saved, but in the long range this is a secondary audience. That is why, as we will see time after time, the bulk of the persecution against Paul and his colleagues comes from the ethnic Jews, not the Gentiles. To win the God-fearing Gentiles, Paul has to take the calculated risk of offending the Jews.

....

17. "The God of this people Israel chose our fathers, and exalted the people when they dwelt as strangers in the land of Egypt, and with an uplifted arm He brought them out of it."

....

Paul stresses two important themes in his introductory remarks: First, the Jews are God's chosen people. This is Paul's point of contact with his synagogue audience, his Jewish credentials. He speaks of **our fathers**. And Paul elaborates on this through verse 22. By this, all should be certain that Paul is not anti-Semitic, although before he is through some of the Jews will begin wondering.

Second, God is a God of power. The phrase **with an uplifted arm** is at times translated "with mighty power." The time of the Exodus, to which Paul refers, was a period of some of the most concentrated displays of divine power in history, and Paul's audience would easily recognize this because they celebrated Passover every year.

God's New Plan for Salvation

After a brief review of Jewish history, Paul shows that the succession of Moses, Samuel, Saul, David and John the Baptist led directly to Jesus who came **"from this man's [David's] seed, according to the promise"** (v. 23). This was a declaration that Jesus was the long-awaited Messiah.

And then came the real shocker:

---

26. "Men and brethren, sons of the family of Abraham, and those among you who fear God, to you the word of this salvation has been sent."

Why was this a shocker? Because in this revelation of God's new plan of salvation, not only are the Jews included, as would be expected, but the Gentile God-fearers are also included: **"those among you who fear God."**

The nonnegotiable theological position of the Jews had been that, as the chosen people of God, they had been given an exclusive channel to God through the Mosaic law. Gentiles who also wanted to find God could do so only by becoming Jews and agreeing to adhere to the law. The former Gentiles, who were now proselytes among the Jews, had done that very thing. But the God-fearers had refused to go that far. Paul seemed to be suggesting what would be an outright heresy to the Jewish rabbis, namely that Gentiles could be saved without becoming Jews.

Here is the heart of the message:

....

38. "Therefore let it be known to you, brethren, that through this Man is preached to you the forgiveness of sins; 39. and by Him everyone who believes is justified from all things from which you could not be justified by the law of Moses."

....

Paul speaks of "the forgiveness of sins." The Jews would consider this the Day of Atonement, which had to be repeated year after year because sins could not be forgiven once and for all. The remission of sins is a vital part of the gospel. Actually, Peter understandably mentions it more frequently than does Paul, for Peter is an apostle to the circumcision—the Jews. In his sermon on Pentecost, Peter speaks of repenting and being baptized in the name of Jesus Christ "for the remission of sins" (2:38), and at the house of Cornelius he says, "whoever believes in Him will receive remission of sins" (10:43). Peter, however, does not go as far as to risk raising the issue that "you could not be justified by the law of Moses" (13:39), although Paul, the apostle to the Gentiles, does. Paul would have known full well that the rabbis could not tolerate such a thought.

Paul also adds a further truth: "everyone who believes is justified from all things." Paul's first recorded sermon bears down on one of Christianity's most important theological truths, *justification by faith.* It is a legal term that implies full acquittal. Once justification takes place it does not need to be repeated time after time. The record is wiped clean. Many would be asking, "Is this fair?" Yes, it is fair because Jesus paid the penalty for sin—death—even though He did not deserve it. Paul later puts it together by saying, "For the wages of sin is death, but the gift of God is eternal life in Christ Jesus our Lord" (Rom. 6:23). We don't deserve it, so it is all by grace. The Jews in Antioch, predictably, were having a difficult time absorbing these things, and the believers among them as well would not all come around quickly, as Paul's epistle to these same Galatians will later show.

Who can be justified? Paul was perfectly clear when he named his two audiences not once, but twice (see Acts 13:16 and 26), as being *both* Jews *and* God-fearers (Gentiles). Then he declared that *everyone* can be justified! The Jews' main message of salvation was "keep the law." Paul's new message of salvation was "believe." Humans constantly attempt to develop ways and means for them to save themselves by *works*. God, on the other hand, wants to save us by *faith*.

The Response to Paul's Message

....

> 42. And when the Jews went out of the synagogue,....
> 43. Now when the congregation had broken up, many
> of the Jews and devout proselytes followed Paul and
> Barnabas, who, speaking to them, persuaded them to
> continue in the grace of God.

....

A two-pronged response came from the Jews. Some of the Jews, including the principal leaders, just **went out of the synagogue.** But they were not passive. They soon took radical action against Paul and Barnabas both verbally and politically.

Many of the common rank-and-file Jews, however, believed in Jesus and were saved. This is the meaning of **persuaded them to continue in the grace of God.** Some of the proselytes were also included among the new believers who would have become what we call today "Messianic Jews."

The enthusiastic positive response came from the Gentile God-fearers:

---

42. And when the Jews went out of the synagogue, the Gentiles begged that these words might be preached to them the next Sabbath.
44. And the next Sabbath almost the whole city came together to hear the word of God.

The Gentiles were ecstatic—Paul's message was better than they could have dreamed! The God-fearers knew that Yahweh was the one true God and they wanted salvation. But they could not bring themselves and their families to break social and cultural ties with their own people, become Jews and adhere to the Jewish law to merit that salvation. Now Paul comes along and removes the only major obstacle, telling them that through faith in Jesus Christ as the Messiah they could be saved without becoming Jews, getting circumcised or obeying the Mosaic law. This was truly good news, the root meaning of "gospel."

This good news would account for the God-fearers coming back on the second Sabbath, but they could have been only a small percentage of the Gentiles in Antioch. What would account for the fact that **the next Sabbath almost the whole city came together to hear the word of God?**

Luke doesn't answer this question directly, so it is up to us to propose what known characteristic of the ministry of Paul and Barnabas could possibly have drawn a whole Gentile city to a public evangelistic service. It is reasonable to conclude that it might well have been that the missionaries characteristically did not minister only in *word*, but also in *deed*. After this ministry trip was over,

Paul and Barnabas met with the Jerusalem Council. Luke's report of the council states: **Then all the multitude kept silent and listened to Barnabas and Paul declaring how many miracles and wonders God had worked through them among the Gentiles (15:12).**

Paul's *words* might have been enough to convince the God-fearers, but it would have been the **miracles and wonders** that most likely would have attracted the rest of Antioch's Gentiles. These were not God-fearers. These were raw pagans who were daily subjected to the fear of the evil spirits that surrounded them and controlled much of their lives. They were not worried so much about their sins, as they were worried about the demonic spirits. The God-fearers wanted justification by faith without the law. The pagans, by far the majority, wanted deliverance from the powers of darkness. Furthermore, they wanted physical healing. They were attracted to a miracle-working God. No matter which avenue they took, Paul was fulfilling his commission **"to open their eyes and to turn them from darkness to light, and from the power of Satan to God"** (26:18).

Paul and Barnabas planted a growing Gentile church, so alive with the power of God that the believers in turn evangelized their whole area:

13:48. Now when the Gentiles heard this, they were glad and glorified the word of the Lord. And as many as had been appointed to eternal life believed. 49. And the word of the Lord was being spread throughout the region.

The Jewish Uprising

45. But when the Jews saw the multitudes, they were filled with envy; and contradicting and blaspheming, they

opposed the things spoken by Paul.

50. But the Jews stirred up the devout and prominent women and the chief men of the city, raised up persecution against Paul and Barnabas, and expelled them from their region.

What had been happening in Antioch was not a trivial thing and the Jewish leaders fully recognized the fact. They did what they could by **contradicting and blaspheming**, but finally they appealed to the powers that be in the Gentile political structure and succeeded **and expelled them from their region**. The Jewish leaders had been thoroughly embarrassed by Paul's popularity, by hearing their theological nonnegotiables soundly contradicted and by the public display of the miraculous power of God that had not operated through them, but through others.

So Paul and Barnabas made a striking public declaration to the Jews:

46. Then Paul and Barnabas grew bold and said, "It was necessary that the word of God should be spoken to you first; but since you reject it, and judge yourselves unworthy of everlasting life, behold, we turn to the Gentiles."
51. But they shook off the dust from their feet against them, and came to Iconium.

This does not mean that, as they moved from place to place, Paul and his mission team no longer preached to Jews. On the contrary, the pattern of starting in the local synagogue established in **Antioch in Pisidia** was continued as a viable mission strategy. But because Paul ministered in similar ways in the future, the reaction was to be similar. The establishment Jews rejected his message with as much violence as they could muster, and the nucleus of the new churches he planted was largely made up of the God-fearing Gentiles. The believers then moved out with the word of God in E-1, or monocultural, evangelism and the Gentile churches multiplied and grew.

But as far as the local situation in Antioch was concerned, the verbal declaration and the prophetic act of shaking dust off their feet, as Jesus had instructed His disciples to do in the face of rejection (see Matt. 10:14), was important to the nucleus of believers Paul and Barnabas had left behind. Thus, Luke is able to report:

13:52. And the disciples were filled with joy and with the Holy Spirit.

Reflection Questions

1. The church at Antioch was unlike many churches we are *p 143* accustomed to today. Review the section that describes the Antioch church and list three or four important characteristics.
2. The words "sodality" and "modality" are new terms for many people. See if you can define them in your own words and then name several sodalities and modalities you know of firsthand. *P 149*
3. Think of sorcerers such as Bar-Jesus. Are they really in touch with a supernatural power that can perform miracles, or are they fakes and deceivers, such as some slight-of-hand illusionists you may know? *P159*
4. Work through the implications of a secular political ruler such as Sergius Paulus receiving power through an occult practitioner and a foreign missionary coming in and challenging that power. Do you think more such power encounters should take place today? *P 155*

Modality (congregational structures)
Sodality (mission structures)

5. Why would Paul's message of justification by faith be good news to the God-fearers, but an incitement to riot to the ethnic Jews? *P163-164 etc*

Notes

1. Everett F. Harrison, *The Apostolic Church* (Grand Rapids: William B. Eerdmans Publishing Co., 1985), p. 186.
2. Dean S. Gilliland, *Pauline Theology and Mission Practice* (Grand Rapids: Baker Book House, 1983), p. 209.
3. C. Peter Wagner, *Your Spiritual Gifts Can Help Your Church Grow* (Ventura, CA: Regal Books, 1979; revised edition, 1994), pp. 229-230.
4. William Mitchell Ramsay, *St. Paul the Traveller and the Roman Citizen* (London: Hodder and Stoughton, 1925), p. 65.
5. Simon J. Kistemaker, *Exposition of the Acts of the Apostles* (Grand Rapids: Baker Book House, 1990), p. 454.
6. F. F. Bruce, *The Book of Acts* (Grand Rapids: William B. Eerdmans Publishing Co., 1954; revised edition, 1988), pp. 245-246.
7. Ralph D. Winter, "The Two Structures of God's Redemptive Mission," *Missiology: An International Review* (January 1974): 121-139.
8. John Stott, *The Spirit, the Church and the World: The Message of Acts* (Downers Grove, IL: InterVarsity Press, 1990), p. 220.
9. Susan R. Garrett, *The Demise of the Devil* (Minneapolis: Fortress Press, 1989), p. 80.
10. Ibid.
11. Ibid.
12. Ibid., p. 84.

CHAPTER

6

Acts 14

Extending God's Kingdom Upsets the Enemy

Somewhere around this time, which was in late A.D. 47 or early 48, Paul was sick. When, a year or so later, he writes his Epistle to the Galatians and addresses it to these very churches, Paul says, "You know that because of physical infirmity I preached the gospel to you at the first" (Gal. 4:13). Luke does not record Paul's sickness in Acts, so it is impossible to pinpoint exactly what the disease was and why it might have forced Paul to go to this particular region. The climate of the area, which was the plateau of the Taurus mountains at 3,600 feet, may have been a factor. Indeed, William Ramsay supposes that Paul might have taken sick in Perga and left hastily to get to the higher and more healthy altitude of Galatia where Antioch of Pisidia was located.[1]

Whatever the full explanation might be, it is remarkable that Paul, in view of his infirmity, had the tremendous combination of energy and character to travel from place to place on foot, sleep wherever he could lie down, face both verbal and physical abuse, and still lead an aggressive church-planting ministry across new frontiers. No wonder so many missionaries through the centuries could identify so closely with Paul. Many have similar biographies.

Through much tribulation, Paul pushes on to Iconium, Lystra and Derbe before turning back and revisiting the new churches.

Iconium

14:1. Now it happened in Iconium that they went together to the synagogue of the Jews,....

Iconium, which is called Konya today, is still in Turkey, about 80 miles east of Antioch of Pisidia. It ordinarily would have taken Paul, Barnabas and the others the better part of a week to make the journey along the well-traveled Roman trade route.

When they arrived in Iconium, they followed their normal pattern of locating the Jewish quarter, establishing themselves there among their own kind of people and attending the synagogue on the Sabbath. As we have seen, they previously did this in Salamis (see 13:5) and in Antioch (see 13:14). We do not know when Paul and Barnabas began to preach in the synagogue, but because they were in Iconium **a long time** (14:3), they likely did not begin preaching the very first Sabbath. It might have been awhile before they were actually invited to preach.

Their audience in the Iconium synagogue would have been made up, as before, of Jews—both ethnic Jews and proselytes—and of Gentiles or God-fearers, whom Luke chooses to refer to in this instance as "Greeks":

> **1.** ...and so spoke that a great multitude both of the Jews
> and of the Greeks believed.

Although Paul is featured as the preacher in Antioch, here in Iconium, apparently, Barnabas also shares the pulpit. But it can be safely assumed that the message of both of them followed the lines of the model given for us in Antioch of Pisidia. The story of their ministry in Antioch took 36 verses for Luke to record, but he uses only 5 verses for Iconium because he apparently believes he does not have to repeat what he had previously said. The next stop, Lystra, will be vastly different.

The results? Here Luke describes the large number of converts: **a great multitude both of the Jews and of the Greeks believed.** Although Paul by now knew that the majority of believers in the nucleus of these new churches would ultimately consist of Gentile God-fearers, initially he also bore substantial fruit among ordinary ethnic Jews. Their unconverted leaders, however, perceived Paul and Barnabas as traitors to the faith of their fathers, so they predictably turned to their influential friends in the Gentile power structure of the city for help:

> **2.** But the unbelieving Jews stirred up the Gentiles
> and poisoned their minds against the brethren.
> **3.** Therefore they stayed there a long time, speaking
> boldly in the Lord, who was bearing witness to the
> word of His grace, granting signs and wonders to be
> done by their hands.

The opposition could not have reached a critical mass too quickly because Paul and Barnabas **stayed there a long time.** Exactly how long we do not know, but it was sufficient time to establish the nucleus of a healthy church. Their ministry while they were there bore much fruit because they ministered both in word and in deed.

Words Are Validated by Deeds

Luke describes Paul and Barnabas's ministry in word as **speaking boldly in the Lord.** This effective preaching did not come about because Paul and Barnabas were extraordinary human orators. We are told of one occasion when a man fell asleep while Paul was preaching (see Acts 20:7-12; 1 Cor. 2:1-5). Nor was it because of their personal magnetism. Indeed, the most detailed physical description we have of Paul comes not from Acts, but from later history when an eyewitness resident of this city of Iconium, named Onesiphorus, is said to describe Paul as follows: "A man small of stature, with a bald head and crooked legs, in a good state of body, with eyebrows meeting and nose somewhat hooked."[2]

The reason Paul's message made such an impression was that he, along with Barnabas, preached **in the Lord.** This was the power of God through the spoken word, to the extent that the same Onesiphorus also says of Paul: "Now he appeared like a man, and now he had the face of an angel."[3] This is another way of saying that the anointing of the Holy Spirit on Paul was at times so powerful, it could be seen as a tangible change in his facial countenance. I have Christian friends today who, like Onesiphorus, have a special ability to see with their physical eyes the power of the Holy Spirit resting on certain people. It is so evident to them, some have a difficult time realizing that not everyone else in the room can see the same evidence. I usually find myself in this latter company, much to the dismay and sometimes irritation of my friends who are seeing it clearly.

But Paul and Barnabas also ministered in deed. The same Lord

who was anointing them with powerful speech was **granting
signs and wonders to be done by their hands.** How was it that
so many pagan Gentiles who were not God-fearers were saved?
Ministry in the word would have been sufficient for the conversion of many of the God-fearers because Paul and Barnabas
brought just the good news they had been waiting for, as I
explained in detail in the last chapter. But in Antioch, practically
the whole city came to the synagogue on the second Sabbath,
not primarily because of the *word*, but because of ministry in
deed.

The same thing was happening here in Iconium. It is not that
signs and wonders have power to save, but the signs and wonders—the deeds—were **bearing witness to the word of His
grace.** Without the signs and wonders the unbelievers would not
have listened so readily to the word, through which they were
saved. It is unfortunate that many of today's preachers and missionaries have turned their backs on this clear biblical dynamic
for evangelism.

Over the period of **a long time,** here is what was happening:

....

**4. But the multitude of the city was divided: part sided
with the Jews, and part with the apostles. 5. And when a
violent attempt was made by both the Gentiles and Jews,
with their rulers, to abuse and stone them, 6. they became
aware of it and fled....**

....

Luke's statement that **a great multitude...believed** (v. 1), and
the subsequent description of the division of the population of
Iconium, give the impression that the percentage of the city that
had become Christian before Paul and Barnabas left was significant. Nevertheless, the opposition prevailed. The phrase **to
abuse and stone them** (v. 5) indicates nothing less than a mur-

der plot against the missionaries. So when they heard through reliable informants that such a plot was about to be implemented, Paul and Barnabas did the prudent thing and left Iconium. They had accomplished their purpose of planting a solid church.

A Different Strategy for Lystra

---

6. They became aware of it and fled to Lystra and Derbe, cities of Lycaonia, and to the surrounding region. 7. And they were preaching the gospel there. 8. And in Lystra....

Lystra was only about a day's journey on foot from Iconium. Paul and Barnabas might not have gone directly there, however, because some time or other they preached also **to the surrounding region**, and they could have spent some time evading their enemies.

Nothing is said of a synagogue in Lystra, and none of the references I have been able to consult suggests that one might have been located there. A scattering of Jews might have been living there, however, because Lystra is the place where Paul later links up with Timothy, whose mother and grandmother were Jewish. Paul and Barnabas likely would have sought out the Jews first, but in this case they sought them out primarily for social rather than strategic reasons. The absence of a synagogue would have also meant the absence, for all intents and purposes, of a significant group of God-fearers who would ordinarily have been Paul's primary target audience, as we have seen.

If their strategy of going to the synagogue first had been well established, why then, would they have stopped at Lystra? No one knows for sure, but one possibility might have been that they were fleeing for their lives and did not have as much a luxury of choice as they had when they went through Perga without stopping, for example. Another possibility might have been that God simply spoke to them in one way or another and told them they were to minister in Lystra and change their strategy accordingly. Behind this is the thought that our missionary strategy, successful as it might prove to be, must always be seen as a means to an end, not as an end in itself. The end is to bring unbelievers into faith in Jesus Christ, and if it requires an adjustment in strategy to make that happen, so be it.

The major adjustment Paul made in Lystra was to assign ministry *in deed* a higher initial priority than ministry *in word*. The word would have been suitable for God-fearers, but, as in Iconium and Antioch, the pagan Gentiles would best be attracted first by the signs and wonders, and only then to the explanation of the gospel of Jesus Christ as Savior and Lord.

The Lame Man Walks

8. And in Lystra a certain man without strength in his feet was sitting, a cripple from his mother's womb, who had never walked. 9. This man heard Paul speaking. Paul, observing him intently and seeing that he had faith to be healed, 10. said with a loud voice, "Stand up straight on your feet!" And he leaped and walked.

We have here in Lystra another specific example of "power evangelism," to use a modern term coined by John Wimber.[4] Power evangelism is evangelistic strategy based primarily on a visible manifestation of the power of God through signs, wonders, miracles and power encounters. Power evangelism was not mentioned specifically in Antioch because Luke's emphasis there was on Paul's spoken message. Nor does Luke mention signs and wonders in connection with the next stop on this missionary trip, Derbe. However, in Iconium Luke specifies that God granted **signs and wonders** (v. 3), but he gives them more prominence here in Lystra.

Everett Harrison concludes that miraculous manifestations "are mentioned [here] only in connection with the mission at Iconium and Lystra, but they must have occurred in the other two cities also."[5] Ernst Haenchen affirms that the wonders of God's power are "a part of God's witness to the Christian proclamation," and because of that, "when in what follows a special miracle is recounted, the reader knows that it is not an isolated event, an exceptional case, but a link in a long chain."[6]

Although Luke here emphasizes the deed, the word is not absent. The lame man first comes on the scene when **this man heard Paul speaking** (v. 9). He is described as **a cripple from his mother's womb, who had never walked** (v. 8). For those who have been active in the ministry of divine healing, as I have been for more than 10 years, the challenge of a person lame from birth comes as a rather extraordinary challenge. Although I have a quasi specialization in healing backs and legs, I have never as yet had the joy of seeing a cripple from birth leap and walk as a consequence of my ministry, although I have prayed for many. This is true of most of my friends. Oh, an Oral Roberts here and a John Wimber or Reinhard Bonkke there have seen them, but they also will say such a thing is extraordinary.

As I write, news of some of the greatest evangelistic harvest in history is coming out of mainland China. Some estimates go up to 35,000 conversions a day. Karen Feaver, who was part of a United States congressional delegation to Beijing, reports that Christian women who came in from Sichuan province told her, "Wherever we go, signs and wonders follow our sisters and brothers." They told her that in one meeting in which no one wanted to hear the gospel they were attempting to preach, a person who had been lame for 70 years got up and walked.[7] Such things actually do happen today, and the evangelistic effectiveness is great.

All Miracles Are Not the Same

All signs and wonders, whether healings or deliverances or nature miracles or power encounters or whatever, are not equal. They are all truly manifestations of the power of God, but some are much more dramatic than others. Likewise, all conversions are produced by God's power, but some, as that of the apostle Paul, are more dramatic than most.

The healing of the lame man in Lystra was clearly one of those considered in the more dramatic category. Who knows how many boils or headaches or colds or fevers or slipped disks were also being healed through the ministry of the apostles? Who also knows how many people Paul and Barnabas prayed for who did not get healed (see 2 Tim. 4:20)? Luke, as all historians before and after, is selective. He chooses what to tell and also what not to tell. Most authors writing about signs and wonders choose the successes, and among them the most dramatic successes, to relate to their readers. I did this, for example, when I wrote my book *How to Have a Healing Ministry in Any Church*, and John Wimber also did it in his book *Power Healing* (HarperSanFrancisco, 1987).

On the other hand, both Wimber and I frankly admit in our books that not all are healed and we attempt to deal responsibly with the issues raised. In my book, I share the statistics that in my personal ministry, and also in Wimber's Vineyard Christian Fellowship, around 20 percent of those to whom we minister show no effects.[8] Although Luke doesn't mention the occasion in his Gospel, Matthew tells us that Jesus experienced such disappointments as well. When in Nazareth, "[Jesus] did not do many mighty works there because of their unbelief" (Matt. 13:58). In designing his Gospel, John carefully chose seven of Jesus' most astounding miracles around which to outline what we call the fourth Gospel, but he mentions no failures.

I say this to point out that simply because Luke does not choose to mention the failures in Paul's and Barnabas's ministry of signs and wonders, some mistakenly suppose that the apostles must have been 100 percent successful. Some of them then move from that rationale, by a kind of curious reasoning, to conclude that the fact that not all are healed today shows that healing ministries in particular and power evangelism in general, although prominent in the first century, are not to be included as part of our missionary strategy. None of this was necessarily the case in Paul's time, nor do I think it is the case today.

Faith in Healing

Paul, **seeing that he had faith to be healed** (Acts 14:9), ministered directly to the lame man. What does this mean? Does this mean that divine healing will take place only when the sick person has enough faith to make it happen?

Obviously, several parallels can be drawn between healing this lame man in Lystra and healing the lame man at the Temple gate in Jerusalem in Acts 3. One of the differences, however, is that in Jerusalem nothing is said or implied that the faith of the lame man had anything to do with the healing.

To review what I mentioned at that point in discussing Acts 3, clearly a biblical relationship can be found between faith and divine healing, admitting also that the sovereign God at times chooses to bypass His ordinary *modus operandi* and heal apart from any known context of faith. The spiritual healing of Saul on the Damascus road would be an example of such divine intervention. But God *usually* moves in His supernatural power in response to faith.

The location of this faith, however, will vary from case to case. In Jerusalem, the faith was present in Peter and John, not in the lame man. When Jesus healed the centurion's servant, the faith was not in the sick servant but in an intermediary, the centurion. Here in Lystra the faith was, in fact, in the sick person, the lame man. To answer our question, then, in some cases the faith of the sick person is a factor in the healing process and in other cases it is not.

Paul had faith as well. He **said with a loud voice, "Stand up straight on your feet!"** (14:10). Presumably guided by the Holy Spirit, Paul decided to use what we call today, for lack of a better term, a "command prayer." The most common form of healing prayer is petition, in which we ask God to do the healing by His Holy Spirit. Another form, which Paul used with the sorcerer Bar-Jesus in West Cyprus, is prayer of rebuke. The command prayer is risky, especially if done in public as we see here, because it presupposes that God has chosen to heal in this particular case and has directed the use of this form of prayer. Paul would have risked public embarrassment and a degree of discrediting his message if he had not heard from God correctly.

But Paul *had* heard from God and the lame man **leaped and walked!**

The Crowd's Reaction

11. Now when the people saw what Paul had done, they raised their voices, saying in the Lycaonian language, "The gods have come down to us in the likeness of men!" 12. And Barnabas they called Zeus, and Paul, Hermes, because he was the chief speaker. 13. Then the priest of Zeus, whose temple was in front of their city, brought oxen and garlands to the gates, intending to sacrifice with the multitudes.

If Paul had been preaching in a synagogue, this incident would never have occurred. Monotheistic Jews would not have reacted the way these Gentiles did. Both Jews and Gentiles in the first century shared a worldview that allowed for the intervention of supernatural power in daily life, unlike many in our modern rationalistic world. They believed in the miraculous, in angels and in demons. But their spiritual bondages were different. As Paul later writes, the god of this age (Satan) had blinded their minds to the gospel (see 2 Cor. 4:4).

Satan blinded the Jews mainly by deceiving them into thinking so highly of the Mosaic law that they could not accept the notion of justification by faith. This became especially clear in Antioch of Pisidia. He did it mainly to the Gentiles by deceiving them into thinking that the demonic principalities that ruled over them and their cities were benign and that he had their best interests in mind. This was especially clear here in Lystra.

Glorifying Principalities of Darkness

Two of the principalities of darkness to which the Lystrans had given special allegiance were the Greek deities Zeus (whom the Romans called Jupiter) and Hermes (whom the Romans called Mercury). The miracle of healing the lame man was so awesome in their eyes that, to explain how it must have happened, they went right to the top. In their minds, this was nothing the lesser spirits, whom they also served and to whom they sacrificed, could possibly have done. So they logically (according to their worldview) assumed Zeus had appeared as Barnabas and Hermes had appeared as Paul. They were grateful for the healing, so they decided to honor the only power they believed could have been strong enough to have caused the miracle.

Do demonic forces ever do good things to people? Of course. Sick people treated by psychics in the Philippines actually get well, some through bloodless, physical surgery. Lonesome men and women find ardent lovers through voodoo in Haiti. Fortune-tellers in Japan warn clients of potential dangers and tell them how to avoid them. In Los Angeles, distraught people learn the precise location of lost items through Santería. Demonic forces are not quaint superstitions of backward, unenlightened people. They are personalities that intervene in daily human life and sometimes have amazing supernatural power. Denying their existence does not neutralize their effectiveness. And although many of their activities take the appearance of being good, such are only deceitful means used by the powers of darkness to accomplish their malignant ends.

The devil and his forces are in the world to steal, to kill and to destroy (see John 10:10). Just as God allows signs and wonders to point people toward eternal life, so Satan permits signs and wonders to point people to eternal death. That is why signs and wonders from God are also means, not ends. That is why the *word* is not optional, but it must accompany the *deed.*

Deceived into thinking that the supernatural power that healed the lame man came from Zeus and Hermes, the Lystran priests were preparing to thank them through the usual means, blood sacrifice. The choice of oxen, rather than smaller animals, seems to indicate the unusual magnitude of the impression the miracle had on the community. To further impress the spirits, beautiful woolen garlands were hung on the bodies of the oxen before offering them to Zeus and Hermes. A large and public affair was taking shape.

Don't Glorify the Creature; Glorify the Creator!

14:14. But when the apostles Barnabas and Paul heard this, they tore their clothes and ran in among the multi-

tude, crying out 15. and saying, "Men, why are you doing
these things? We also are men with the same nature as
you, and preach to you that you should turn from these
vain things to the living God, who made the heaven, the
earth, the sea, and all things that are in them, 16. who in
bygone generations allowed all nations to walk in their
own ways. 17. Nevertheless He did not leave Himself
without witness, in that He did good, gave us rain from
heaven and fruitful seasons, filling our hearts with food
and gladness."

....

History indicates that the Lystrans would have been bilingual, by
and large. Lycaonian was their native tongue, but the trade language of that part of the Roman Empire was Greek. Paul and
Barnabas had been preaching and conversing with the Lystrans
in Greek. When the excitement about the miraculous healing
swept the city, however, the Lystrans naturally reverted to their
heart language, and Luke specifically tells us **they raised their
voices, saying in the Lycaonian language** (14:11).

The missionaries couldn't understand Lycaonian so they may
have been unaware of what was actually transpiring. If they had
known, we can assume they would have attempted to abort the
pagan worship ceremony before it got as far as it did. It could
have been the appearance of the oxen with their ceremonial garlands around their necks that tipped off the apostles about what
was really happening.

As soon as Paul and Barnabas found out the meaning of the
ceremony, however, they were appalled. They took immediate
and decisive action. They wanted no part of any pagan sacrifice
that involved them either as sacrificers or sacrificees. Although,
as strangers, they had no special influence in the city, their tem-
porary role as perceived incarnations of deity gave them enough

authority to persuade the people not to follow through. It was no easy task, however, because at the end of the episode, Luke writes:

....

18. And with these sayings they could scarcely restrain the multitudes from sacrificing to them.

....

Three verses (14:15-17) constitute a brief summary of one of two recorded messages Paul preached to pagan Gentiles who were not God-fearers. The other verse will be revealed in Athens in Acts 17. Paul's main theme for the Lystrans could not be that Jesus is the Messiah fulfilling Old Testament revelation, because they would not so much as have heard of the Old Testament. Paul's message here could be summed up in the words of Joshua: "Choose for yourselves this day whom you will serve" (Josh. 24:15).

Previously, the Lystrans had served Zeus, whom they had invited to be the patron deity over the city. A temple for the worship of Zeus stood right outside the city. They also worshiped the messenger of Zeus, Hermes, to whom they had erected a statue, dedicating the statue to Zeus. For who knows how long, the Lystrans had served these two territorial principalities of darkness along with all the members of the hierarchy of evil under them who had been assigned by Satan to keep the Lystrans in spiritual captivity. This wasn't something marginal to their existence. As is common with animistic peoples everywhere, subservience to these dark angels was part of their conscious daily routine from morning to night. They had never known anything different. But the missionaries had come to offer them a better option.

When the Issue Is Power, Not Knowledge

The issue here is not knowledge. People who have an animistic

worldview cannot be reasoned into conversion. The issue is power.
Is this new God, the Father of the Lord Jesus Christ, more powerful
than Zeus and Hermes? This is the question Paul was addressing.

The reason Paul could address this issue of power was the healing of the lame man. Chances are, no miracle of this magnitude
had previously been seen in Lystra. By stopping the sacrifice, Paul
and Barnabas had succeeded in persuading the crowd that the
power that had healed the lame man was not the power of Zeus
and Hermes. From the Lystrans' point of view, if the supernatural
power had not come from Zeus, who was the chief of all the gods
of the Greek pantheon, it must have come from a yet higher
source they were hearing about for the first time.

Who was this God who had so much power?

Paul revealed to them that God was **"the living God, who
made the heaven, the earth, the sea, and all things that are in
them"** (Acts 14:15). God was nothing less than the Creator—by
implication, the Creator also of Zeus and Hermes. Paul's
approach to the Lystrans was what Charles Kraft calls an "allegiance encounter."[9] In this instance it was not a "truth
encounter," as it was in Antioch where the issue was grace versus
law. Nor was it a "power encounter," as it was in West Cyprus
with Bar-Jesus representing Satan versus Paul representing God.
God had shown His superior power, so the Lystrans were faced
with the decision whether they should give up their allegiance to
Zeus and Hermes and switch it to Jesus Christ.

Knowing the Old Testament and the gospel, the issue foremost
in Paul's mind was that these Lystrans were glorifying the creature (Zeus and Hermes) rather than the Creator. Throughout the
Bible, chapter by chapter and book by book, this is by far the sin
that upsets God more than any other. It is no mere happenstance
that the first two of the Ten Commandments deal with this issue:
(1) "You shall have no other gods before Me" and (2) "You shall

not make for yourself any carved image" (Exod. 20:3,4). Paul uses the same theme when he speaks to other pagan Gentiles later in Athens (see Acts 17:24-27), and then he elaborates on the theme in detail in Romans 1 where he says, "[They] worshiped and served the creature rather than the Creator" (Rom. 1:25).

What were the results? How many chose to serve God rather than Zeus and Hermes? How many took Paul's advice to **"turn from these vain things"** (Acts 14:15)? Luke does not stop to give us a church growth report here in Lystra as he does in many other places. What we do know from verse 20 is that some Christian disciples were made, and from subsequent visits of Paul to Lystra we also know that a solid church had been planted. We can only wish we had more information about the numbers.

Paul Is Raised from the Dead

19. Then Jews from Antioch and Iconium came there; and having persuaded the multitudes, they stoned Paul and dragged him out of the city, supposing him to be dead. 20. However, when the disciples gathered around him, he rose up and went into the city....

We may not know how many disciples had been made in Lystra, but the news of Paul's ministry there reached Iconium where Paul was still under sentence of death. The unbelieving Jews, both in Iconium and Antioch of Pisidia, which was 100 miles away, were the instigators of the persecutions, convincing Gentile political leaders in both places that Paul and the others should be declared persona non grata. When they discovered Paul's whereabouts, they came to Lystra and accomplished the same thing.

When the unbelieving Jews arrived in Lystra, they **persuaded the multitudes** that they should be allowed to carry out Paul's prescribed execution. Presumably, Paul was captured by the local security forces, and the Jews from Iconium and Antioch proceeded with their public stoning. Their purpose was to kill Paul as other Jews had done to Stephen.

Did they succeed? Was Paul really dead? The commentators I have access to assume that because Paul left Lystra alive the next day, he couldn't really have been dead. Awhile back, when we were looking at Peter raising Dorcas from the dead in Acts 9, I pointed out that a common explanation of reports of dead being raised today is that they could not have really been dead, but they only appeared to be dead. I am not suggesting that such a thing as a mistaken diagnosis does not occur, and this may very well be the explanation in some cases; but not in all cases.

Was Paul Really Dead?

It is safe to say that Dorcas was really dead, because Luke, a physician, tells us clearly that she was (see 9:37). Luke does not say this directly about Paul here in Lystra, however, so conclusions, accordingly, must be more tentative. My own conclusion from the information we have is that in all probability Paul was really dead, and that he was miraculously raised from the dead when the disciples gathered around him in prayer.

How do I come to this conclusion?

To start with, and most commentators would agree on this point, it is possible that a person can be dead and subsequently, through the supernatural power of God, be brought back to life. For example, Lazarus was raised by God's power after four days and his body smelled of rotting tissue. Paul's being raised from the dead is, therefore, at least within the scope of biblical possibilities.

Second, the Jews who were carrying out the execution presumably had prior experience in meting out capital punishment. They knew how to stone a person and they knew how to stone

one to death. The fact that they had stoned Paul inside the city, then **dragged him [his body] out of the city**, indicates that they were handling a corpse. We need not speculate whether these fanatical Jews knew the difference between death and life. No wonder they [supposed] him to be dead.

The question remains: Why didn't Luke say so? I believe he did say so, indirectly. But apart from that, Luke was still a historian and, as we have seen on many occasions, he picks and chooses what he decides to put into print. The fact that he did not write about signs and wonders in Antioch of Pisidia, for example, is no reason to assume they did not happen there. Ernst Haenchen points out that one of the notable things about Luke's writings is his inclination toward "playing down these *pathemata*,"[10] or sufferings of the apostles. If this is true, it could be a reasonable explanation of Luke's desire to move on rapidly to the evangelistic ministry in the next stop, Derbe.

Luke may not have stressed Paul's sufferings, but Paul himself was not inhibited from writing about them, at least on occasion. Although we will never know for sure, it could well be that he flashed back to this event in Lystra when he later wrote to the Corinthians, "Once I was stoned" (2 Cor. 11:25), also affirming that he was "in deaths often" (v. 23).

Just as an aside, many associate Paul's out-of-the-body experience in the third heaven, which he relates in 2 Corinthians 12:2-4, with this execution by stoning in Lystra. However, Paul writes about that incident happening "fourteen years ago" (v. 2). Because he wrote 2 Corinthians in A.D. 54 or possibly as late as 57, and this visit to Lystra occurred no earlier than 47, the evidence does not seem to support this conclusion.

Imagine the joy of the new disciples in Lystra when they gathered around Paul's corpse, which had been dragged outside the city, and watched as **he rose up** (Acts 14:20)!

Raising the Dead Today

It may help us in imagining such an incident to remind ourselves that similar things also happen today. Just two days ago, as I write this, my friend Larry Lea told me of an experience he had the previous week in Chicago. He was on the platform of a church meeting for an evening service and just as the time was approaching for Larry to deliver his message, a disturbance of some kind was noticed near the rear of the large auditorium. Word came to the platform that a woman, well known in the congregation, had collapsed and was taken to a room near the church entrance. She was being attended by a medical doctor, also from the congregation, and the emergency paramedics had been called along with an ambulance. Right after Larry had been introduced and had begun to speak, word came to the platform that the woman had died!

Few guest speakers have been faced with such a challenge. What could he say to a congregation, now swept by group trauma and many weeping, handkerchiefs in hand? Rising to the occasion, Larry Lea reminded the congregation that they all could be comforted because Jesus is the Resurrection and the Life. Their friend would be in Jesus' presence and ultimately participate in the resurrection of the dead. He called back the worship team, had the congregation stand, and began to lead a protracted time of worship and praise. He said to me later that it had not occurred to him at the time that the concept of Jesus as the Resurrection and the Life was also attached to the biblical passage telling of Lazarus being raised from the dead.

After 15 minutes or so of continuous praise, another message was delivered to the platform. They had removed the woman's body from the church and were laying it out on the surface where it could be processed. As they did so, the woman opened her eyes and was very much alive! The congregation was ecstatic, just as the disciples in Lystra must have been, and God was glorified.

Although the woman had been pronounced dead by a medical doctor and the paramedics, some may suggest she never was really dead in the first place. Likewise, some commentators suppose that Paul was not really dead in Lystra. But at the end of the day, it doesn't really make that much difference. Whether Paul was dead or not, he was physically in critical condition. The brutal stoning had wounded his body considerably, causing cuts, bruises and possibly broken bones. The fact that **the next day he departed with Barnabas to Derbe** (14:20) represented, at the very minimum, an extraordinarily miraculous healing and restoration, which Luke also chooses not to emphasize. But the new disciples had been thoroughly convinced that the God they had decided to follow, instead of Zeus and Hermes, was a God of unsurpassed power who could save them and save their friends. They had turned **"from darkness to light, and from the power of Satan to God"** (26:18). The missionaries' goal had been accomplished and a Christian church had been planted in Lystra.

Derbe

....

14:20. ...And the next day he departed with Barnabas to Derbe. 21. And when they had preached the gospel to that city and made many disciples,....

....

Luke leaves many things to our imagination concerning the ministry of Paul and Barnabas in Derbe. Derbe was a city about 60 miles from Lystra. It would have been a journey of three days or so for the missionaries. Was a synagogue located in Derbe? How long did they stay? What was the nature of their ministry in Derbe?

We know for certain that **they...preached the gospel to that city**. It is interesting that the city itself is mentioned as the target, although Paul was preaching to *people*. In recent times, cities have risen to the top of the agendas of many missionary strategists concerned with completing the Great Commission. Urban evangelism is receiving great attention. More and more Christian leaders, particularly those on the cutting edge of the growing movement for prayer and spiritual warfare, are becoming involved in, to borrow the title of John Dawson's excellent book *Taking Our Cities for God* (Creation House, 1989). This is not to ignore or downplay the value of reaching individuals or families for Christ, but it is to say that something in the heart of God desires entire cities to recognize Jesus Christ as Lord of all, turning to God from their former allegiances to such wicked spirits as Zeus and Hermes.

We can safely assume that the ministry of the apostles in Derbe followed the patterns previously laid down in Antioch, Iconium and Lystra. If Derbe had a synagogue, they would have started there, preaching to the God-fearers. If not, they would have approached the Gentiles with power evangelism, expecting signs and wonders to confirm the validity of the message of Jesus Christ. In any case [preaching] the gospel to that city would have involved ministries of both word and deed.

It is interesting that Luke mentions no persecution in Derbe. This could have been because of the brevity of his account, which is only 14 words long. But more likely, no persecution occurred because when Paul later writes to Timothy, he speaks of "persecutions, afflictions, which happened to me at Antioch, at Iconium, at Lystra—what persecutions I endured" (2 Tim. 3:11). Here Paul mentions the other three cities, but not Derbe. It could have been that the absence of persecution allowed them to stay in Derbe for some time while things were cooling off in Antioch, Iconium and Lystra. In any case, what Everett Harrison says must have been true: "To have a peaceful mission here was a blessing after the stoning in Lystra."[11]

Back to Enemy Territory

....

14:21. ...they returned to Lystra, Iconium, and Antioch,
22. strengthening the souls of the disciples, exhorting them to continue in the faith, and saying, "We must through many tribulations enter the kingdom of God."

....

Although they might have been in Derbe for a long enough time to have things settle down in the cities where they had been brutally persecuted, returning there would have been no easy decision. William Ramsay says, "New magistrates had now come into office in all the cities whence they had been driven."[12] Even so, the unbelieving Jews who had initiated the persecutions would still be there, at least in Iconium and Antioch. If they had persecuted once, what would keep them from doing it again? Returning so soon to these hotbeds of enemy opposition would have taken no little courage.

Why, then, would Paul and Barnabas do such a thing as to return to enemy territory? If they had pushed forward instead of retracing their steps, in a week or so they could have arrived in Tarsus, Paul's hometown. Wouldn't it have been much safer and more pleasant to spend some time with relatives and visit old friends in Tarsus?

Visiting Paul's hometown might have been more pleasant, but it would not have been good missionary strategy. What had taken place on this trip was not just routine church planting, but the sparking of people movements. At least Luke's language points in that direction. In Antioch, **almost the whole city came together to hear the word of God** (13:44). In Iconium, **a great multitude** both of the Jews and of the Greeks believed (14:1). In Derbe, they made many disciples (14:21). An indispensable part of people-movement strategy is postbaptismal care.

Classical missiologist Donald McGavran, the prime theoretician of people movements, says, "The quality of people-movement churches is uniquely dependent on postbaptismal care. In these movements relatively large numbers of converts form new churches quickly. If they are neglected...a starved and nominal membership can be confidently expected." McGavran goes on to say that contrariwise, "If new congregations are nurtured with imagination and faithfulness, in ways that lead their members to a genuine advance in Christian living, solid congregations of sound Christians will result."[13] This is exactly what Paul and Barnabas had in mind when they decided to run the risk of retracing their steps.

Kingdom Work Brings Conflict

The one part of the teaching Paul and Barnabas were giving to the new churches to "lead their members to a genuine advance in Christian living," as McGavran would say, is recorded by Luke as, "We must through many tribulations enter the kingdom of God" (v. 22). As I have said previously, preaching the kingdom of God must be recognized as an invasion of territories previously held by Satan in his kingdom of darkness. Taking people from darkness to light requires spiritual warfare. Satan does not release his captives without a fight. As in any other kind of warfare, spiritual warfare also involves conflict and casualties.

Jesus said the Kingdom of heaven comes with violence "and the violent take it by force" (Matt. 11:12). When He told His disciples He would build His church (see 16:18), He immediately warned them that it would involve spiritual warfare by saying, "And the gates of Hades shall not prevail against it" (16:18). Jesus then went on to say that the keys to advancing His kingdom would be "whatever you bind on earth will be bound in heaven" (16:19). The Greek word for "to bind," *deo*, is the same verb Jesus uses when He speaks of "binding the strong man" in Matthew 12:29.

In these cities in Galatia, Paul was discovering what the spiritual warfare associated with frontier evangelism would look like in practice. He later writes, "For we do not wrestle against flesh and blood, but against principalities, against powers, against the rulers of the darkness of this age, against spiritual hosts of wickedness in the heavenly places" (Eph. 6:12). Paul then describes the armor of God we have been given through the Holy Spirit to move forward and push the enemy out of cities such as Iconium and Lystra. The analogy comes from the Roman legions that were constantly extending the borders of the Roman Empire. Their posture was always offensive. The defensive parts of the armor were only for protection, while openings were being made for cutting down the enemy with the sword—for the Christian the sword of the Spirit is the Word of God (see 6:17).

Paul and Barnabas were teaching the new believers that even in the face of surefire opposition, they were not to huddle back in a defensive posture but were to move aggressively against the forces of the enemy. And they did not hesitate to say that doing this would inevitably involve tribulation. Paul later prayed that the believers in Thessalonica "may be counted worthy of the kingdom of God, for which you also suffer" (2 Thess. 1:5). Paul told Timothy that "all who desire to live godly in Christ Jesus will suffer persecution" (2 Tim. 3:12). Extending God's kingdom definitely upsets the enemy.

Installing the Elders

14:23. So when they had appointed elders in every church, and prayed with fasting, they commended them to the Lord in whom they had believed.

The first time through Antioch, Iconium, Lystra and Derbe, Paul and Barnabas's major goal was to win converts and form them into churches. The second time through Antioch, their major goal was to install the leadership of the churches. Few realize the critical importance of selecting leaders to assure that the fruit of evangelism is also fruit that remains. In many parts of the world today, evangelism is taking place with unbelievable rapidity, but those who give their lives to the Lord do not always become the responsible members of local churches. They too often drift into nominality or dual allegiance, or they leave the Word of God and return to their idols. The skills involved in selecting and training church leaders on the mission fields of the world are without question the most important skills missionaries can take to most fields today.

The Priority of Leadership

We have an excellent model of the high priority of church leadership here in the missionary work of Paul and Barnabas. The timing is notable. Within a very short period of time they appointed elders. They did not set up a training institution and base leadership upon receiving a diploma. They did not require full maturity in the Christian life. They, as outsiders, did not assume the leadership themselves. They did not offer a financial subsidy to support the new leaders. I mention these things because all of the above are built into the very policies of some modern missionary organizations.

What was Paul looking for when he visited the new churches? I believe that, as he later wrote in Romans, 1 Corinthians and Ephesians, he was looking for spiritual gifts. The people in the churches who by then had been recognized as having spiritual gifts, such as the gift of leadership or the gift of pastor or the gift of teaching or other gifts that would qualify them as elders of the local church, were the ones Paul and Barnabas would appoint. Keep in mind that by now the normal first-century pattern of networks of house churches spreading through the cities would have been in progress. None of the cities would have had only one local Christian congregation, but several. Each one needed leaders and, also among all the churches as a group, certain people with gifts of apostle or gifts of prophecy would be recognized. At this time, however, they **appointed elders in every church** (14:23), that is, in every one of the local house churches.

Some may think that church leaders should not be appointed so hastily. In modern missions, however, our error has usually been waiting too long to appoint leaders of the national churches rather than doing it too hastily. It is of interest that a whole new genre of churches is arising today, in every part of the world, that seem much more like the New Testament churches than the traditional churches and missions we have become used to. One characteristic of these churches, which some people call "postdenominational" churches, is that few of their leaders have been trained in Western or Western-derived institutions. Most have been appointed to leadership as mature adults right from the grass roots, just as were the elders in Antioch, Iconium, Lystra and Derbe.

It will come as a surprise to some to learn that a rapidly growing number of modern cross-cultural missionaries are simple believers. The house churches of mainland China are a foremost example of the postdenominational churches. Many of their pastors are illiterate. Few have seen the inside of a college, or any kind of training institution for that matter. Some have never owned a Bible. But not only have they been multiplying churches across China at a remarkable rate, they have also begun to tool up to move into other countries. Some, near the border of Russia, are learning the Russian language so they can move out in cross-cultural missionary work. Others, in a Muslim region of China, are forming a grassroots mission agency to send out Chinese missionaries to the Muslim nations to the west of them. One woman missionary from the Himalayas cannot read, write or count, but she sings the gospel and has made thousands of converts from Hinduism.

By saying this, I am not disparaging quality education. As a seminary professor myself, I am personally dedicated to providing education for as many people as possible. At the same time, however, I fully recognize that God is not limited to seminary graduates for the extension of His kingdom. God is not limited today, and He certainly was not limited in the first century.

Risks in Selecting Church Leaders

Is risk involved in installing national church leadership from the very start? Of course, but Paul was willing to take the risk. The results in Galatia were not all that good. As we will see in the next chapter, Paul had to write one of his most harsh and outspoken epistles to these leaders soon after he and Barnabas left. He then referred to them as "foolish Galatians!" (Gal. 3:1). But that did not reverse his missionary strategy. He kept appointing leaders in the new churches as he had done here in Galatia.

At the ordination procedures, to use a modern term, they always **prayed with fasting** (Acts 14:23). Paul would have depended a great deal on hearing from God through prayer regarding the people the Holy Spirit had gifted and chosen to lead the churches. Undoubtedly, some of the choices were easier than others because the elders had already been recognized as leaders and the people in the congregations were gladly following them. Some may have been more difficult to choose. The choices would always have been made on the assumption that the local church members would have a consensus about who should be their leader. Paul and Barnabas would not have functioned as arbitrary spiritual overlords who superimposed their will on sometimes reluctant churches. But they were apostles, and the Holy Spirit anointed their apostolic authority.

Back to the Base: Antioch

26. From there they sailed to Antioch, where they had been commended to the grace of God for the work which they had completed. 27. And when they had come and gathered the church together, they reported all that God had done with them, and that He had opened the door of faith to the Gentiles. 28. So they stayed there a long time with the disciples.

This had been a strenuous term of missionary service, and Paul and Barnabas were ready for a furlough. They went back to Antioch of Syria and **stayed there a long time with the disciples.** In Antioch was based the headquarters of what I have been calling the Cyprus and Cyrene Mission (CCM), which had sent them out and in all probability supported them. The missionaries would naturally have called together the believers from the many house churches in Antioch to share **all that God had done with them.** They undoubtedly met frequently with them in various parts of the city. They were particularly eager to share that God **had opened the door of faith to the Gentiles** because it was here in Antioch that the first Gentile churches had been planted, as we saw in Acts 11.

Paul and Barnabas were in Antioch for about a year, and during that time the crucial theological issues, concerning whether

Gentiles could truly be saved without being circumcised and becoming Jews, came to a head and needed to be resolved once and for all.

Reflection Questions

1. The healing of the lame man in Lystra apparently was something other than an "ordinary" miracle. Is it proper to speak of some miracles as "ordinary" and others as "extraordinary"? Could you give examples from your own experience? *p 177*

2. In evangelizing Lystra, on the cutting edge of missionary penetration were deeds such as healings and miracles rather than preaching sermons. Can you think of any place in the world today where the same thing might apply? *p 177*

3. What is your opinion of whether or not Paul was actually raised from the dead? Why would your answer cause disagreement? *He was dead*

4. Persecution was severe for the missionaries on their trip. Think of missionaries today in dangerous areas of the world. When should they leave and when should they stay, despite the danger to themselves or to their families? *w God say*

5. The way elders (or pastors) were named and put into leadership positions over the churches in the days of Paul and Barnabas was vastly different from the methods most churches use today. Is it best for us to maintain the status quo or should we make some changes? *p 194*

Notes

1. William Mitchell Ramsay, St. *Paul the Traveller and the Roman Citizen* (London: Hodder and Stoughton, 1925), p. 93.

2. This comes from *Acts of Paul* 3.3, referenced by F. F. Bruce, *The Book of Acts* (Grand Rapids: William B. Eerdmans Publishing Co., 1954; revised edition, 1988), p. 271.

3. Ibid.

4. See John Wimber and Kevin Springer, *Power Evangelism* (San Francisco: HarperSanFrancisco, 1985; revised edition, 1992).

5. Everett F. Harrison, *Acts: The Expanding Church* (Chicago: Moody Press, 1975), p. 219.

6. Ernst Haenchen, *The Acts of the Apostles* (Philadelphia: The Westminster Press, 1971), p. 423.

7. Karen M. Feaver, "What Chinese Christians Taught a U.S. Congressional Delegation," *Christianity Today* (16 May 1994): 34.

8. C. Peter Wagner, *How to Have a Healing Ministry in Any Church* (Ventura, CA: Regal Books, 1988), pp. 243-244.

9. For the important distinction between "power encounter," "truth encounter" and "allegiance encounter," see Charles H. Kraft, "Allegiance, Truth and Power Encounters in Christian Witness," *Pentecost, Mission and Ecumenism Essays on Intercultural Theology*, ed. by Jan A. B. Jongeneel (Frankfurt am Main, Germany: Peter Lang, 1992), pp. 215-230.

10. Haenchen, *The Acts of the Apostles*, p. 434.

11. Harrison, *Acts: The Expanding Church*, p. 225.

12. Ramsay, *St. Paul the Traveller*, p. 120.

13. Donald A. McGavran, *Understanding Church Growth* (Grand Rapids: William B. Eerdmans Publishing Co., 1970; 1980; third edition revised and edited by C. Peter Wagner, 1990), pp. 247-248.

Solving Conflicts in a Multicultural Church

It may seem unusual to find a chapter on Paul's Epistle to the Galatians in the middle of a commentary on Acts. No other commentator of whom I am aware does this, although Ernst Haenchen does allot four pages to Galatians. I am attempting a whole chapter here, not to distract the reader from the sequence of events Luke is describing in the Acts of the Apostles, but the opposite. I do not believe we can gain a full understanding of what Luke describes in Acts 15 without first being aware of the underlying situation that provokes calling an unprecedented summit meeting of church leaders at the Council of Jerusalem.

At the end of the last chapter, we left Paul and Barnabas on furlough in their home base of Antioch of Syria after serving their first term as missionaries in Cyprus and Galatia. They had planted at least four churches in Galatia in the cities of Antioch of Pisidia, Iconium, Lystra and Derbe. Because those churches were in all probability self-propagating churches, considerably more than four churches may have been in existence in the region by this time. The churches were not only self-propagating, but as good indigenous churches they were also self-governing. Paul and Barnabas had gone back to each of the churches and installed elders. I mentioned then that it is sound missionary policy to appoint indigenous leaders in new churches, but that the risks involved should not be ignored. One of the risks, obviously, is that because of the immaturity of the new elders, they are more vulnerable than most to being influenced by unhealthy deviations in doctrine and practice.

A Worst-Case Scenario

What must have been Paul's worst-case scenario had unfolded in these new churches while Paul and Barnabas were on furlough. More rapidly than they would have expected, some church leaders from Jerusalem had visited the Galatian churches without the consent of either Paul or Barnabas and they began contradicting the essence of the message of salvation Paul had preached to the God-fearers and other Gentiles.

This may well have been going on for several weeks or months without Paul and Barnabas knowing anything about it. The bad news surfaced when some of these people, or others who were affiliated with them in Jerusalem, finally arrived in Antioch where the missionaries themselves were staying. Here is how Luke describes it:

....

Acts 15:1. And certain men came down from Judea and taught the brethren, "Unless you are circumcised according to the customs of Moses, you cannot be saved."

....

This was the year A.D. 48. We need to recall that the first Gentile churches had been planted here in Antioch, by what I have chosen to call the Cyprus and Cyrene Mission, in A.D. 45. Uncircumcised Gentiles at that time were professing to be true believers in Jesus Christ, the Son of Jehovah, God of the Jews. This notion was so radical to the majority of born-again Messianic Jewish brothers and sisters that it was totally unacceptable. Previous to that, no believers had been uncircumcised with the exception of those of the house of Cornelius in Caesarea, which was so numerically insignificant that few had paid much attention to it.

In Antioch, however, it seemed as if a movement could be starting. The immediate response of the Jerusalem leaders had been to send Barnabas to Antioch to evaluate the situation. Barnabas liked what he saw, and he "encouraged them all that with purpose of heart they should continue with the Lord" (Acts 11:23). Barnabas stayed on in Antioch to minister to the newly saved Gentiles and then recruited Paul to come from Tarsus and join the Cyprus and Cyrene Mission.

Ethnocentric Christians

Apparently, however, the word Barnabas had sent back to the leaders of the church in Jerusalem had not been fully accepted. As I have pointed out many times, the believers in Jerusalem were saved, they were growing in the Lord, they were filled with the Holy Spirit, they were people of prayer, they were generous with their material goods, and yet they remained monocultural, even ethnocentric, Jews. Salvation does not erase ethnicity, and the subsequent sanctification of ethnic biases and prejudices has seemed through history to take longer than maturity in many other areas of the Christian life.

My point is that the controversial phenomenon of Gentile salvation was only three or four years old at this time, from A.D. 45, when the first Gentile churches were planted, to A.D. 48. The conflicts that had been surfacing were not at all surprising. It would have been more surprising if they had *not* arisen.

Paul was very upset with the ethnocentric Messianic Jews from Jerusalem who came to see them in Antioch, and he told them they were wrong. He was more upset when somehow the news got back from the new churches in Antioch of Pisidia, Iconium, Lystra and Derbe that these people called "Judaizers" had traveled so far and had succeeded in deceiving some of the Gentile believers. The word "Judaizer" is not a biblical word, but it is commonly used to label those who were teaching young Gentile believers that to truly be saved they had to be circumcised and become Jews. Some Bible versions call them "the circumcision party." In my *New King James Version*, Luke describes them as "those of the circumcision who believed" (Acts 10:45).

Two extremely important developments took place at this time: (1) the face-to-face theological debate between Paul and the Judaizers in Antioch sparked the convening of the Jerusalem Council, which we will look at in the next chapter; and (2) the unsettling news from the new churches provoked Paul to write his first epistle, the Epistle to the Galatians, which we will discuss here in some detail. My intention is not to comment on the whole book of Galatians, but to highlight only those points that will help us understand Acts more thoroughly.

For those who may be aware of some of the academic issues relating to Galatians, it will be obvious that I am assuming what is known as the "South Galatian Hypothesis." This means that, in contrast to a North Galatian theory that puts the date of the Epistle to the Galatians much later, I believe it was written to the churches in south Galatia that Paul and Barnabas had just planted. Biblical scholar Ronald Fung assures us that, as far as the English-speaking world is concerned, the South Galatian hypothesis "is followed by the majority of modern interpreters."[1]

Furthermore, I am aware that some scholars have not agreed that the troublemakers in the churches of Galatia were misguided Jewish believers. Some think they might have been unsaved Galatian Jews, some think they were Gentile believers, some think they were gnostics. Without discussing the pros and cons of these theories, as does Ronald Fung, I will simply affirm my agreement with his conclusion: "We take the Galatian agitators to be Jewish Christians who adopted a rigorist attitude towards Gentile Christians and sought to impose upon them circumcision and observance of the law as conditions necessary for salvation or—what amounts to the same thing—for a full Christian status."[2]

Judaizers Preach a Different Gospel

Several passages from Galatians put Paul's view of the problem in clear perspective:

> **Gal. 1:6. I marvel that you are turning away so soon from Him who called you in the grace of Christ, to a different gospel, 7. which is not another; but there are some who trouble you and want to pervert the gospel of Christ.**

The message of the Judaizers was not just another legitimate option to consider, as some might regard being a Baptist or a Presbyterian or a Pentecostal today. It was much more serious than that. Paul calls it a different gospel.

To understand why he does this, flash back to Paul's ministry in Antioch of Pisidia described earlier in chapter 5 of this book. In his sermon in the synagogue in Antioch (Paul's first recorded sermon), he preached that justification was by faith. He said they "could not be justified by the law of Moses" (Acts 13:39), but that forgiveness of sins comes through Jesus Christ and "by Him everyone who believes is justified" (v. 39). Salvation comes by faith, not by works, Paul said. This so infuriated the Jewish leaders in Antioch that they persuaded the municipal authorities to decree Paul's death by stoning. The Jews couldn't handle Paul's doctrine that Gentiles could be saved without first becoming Jews.

The foundational nucleus of the church at Antioch was made up of Gentiles who had become Christians and elders in the church without being circumcised. Then the Judaizers arrive after Paul leaves and tell them that salvation by faith is incomplete, and that only through doing good works, such as circumcision and keeping the law, will God accept them into His family. No wonder Paul is furious:

> **Gal. 1:9. As we have said before, so now I say again, if anyone preaches any other gospel to you than what you have received, let him be accursed.**

Strong language! The word **accursed** means to be delivered to destruction by God. It is the same word Paul later uses when he agonizes so passionately about the fact that the Jews in general were rejecting Christ, and he says, "I could wish that I myself were accursed from Christ for my brethren" (Rom. 9:3). To put it more bluntly, Paul was asking God to do away with these perverters of the true gospel!

Paul describes the Judaizers as:

> **Gal. 2:4. ...false brethren secretly brought in (who came in by stealth to spy out our liberty which we have in Christ Jesus, that they might bring us into bondage), 5. to whom we did not yield submission even for an hour, that the truth of the gospel might continue with you.**

Does Paul call into question the salvation of these Judaizers? The phrase **false brethren** might indicate it. The fact that they were **secretly brought in** and **came in by stealth** seems to point to some kind of conspiracy. Whatever the case, the Judaizers had an unusual amount of influence to which Peter ultimately submitted. Paul does not say it in so many words, but we are here witnessing a powerful counterattack against the spread of the gospel by Satan's forces. If the enemy could be successful in undercutting the doctrine of justification by faith, he could effectively seal off the Christian movement as a mere Jewish cult limited forever to a tiny segment of the earth's population. He could have nullified Jesus' desire that "this gospel of the kingdom will be preached in all the world as a witness to all the nations" (Matt. 24:14).

Paul Versus Peter

Paul's forthright description of his conflict with Peter regarding Gentile conversion is one of those examples of biblical honesty that gives us hope today. In the midst of many of the struggles we ourselves experience in attempting to live out our Christian faith, it is somewhat reassuring to know that apostles such as Paul and Peter did not always see eye to eye either. Paul had to be deeply upset when not only Peter, but also his fellow missionary Barnabas, broke ranks with him during his furlough time in Antioch. Here is what Paul writes:

Gal. 2:11. But when Peter had come to Antioch, I withstood him to his face, because he was to be blamed;
12. for before certain men came from James, he would eat with the Gentiles; but when they came, he withdrew and separated himself, fearing those who were of the circumcision. 13. And the rest of the Jews also played the

> hypocrite with him, so that even Barnabas was
> carried away with their hypocrisy.

Why would Peter do this? Why would he change his behavior?
The first time Peter had eaten with Gentiles was in the house of Cornelius. This was in response to the clear vision God had given him by lowering a sheet filled with nonkosher food and inviting Peter to eat it. Then, when in Cornelius's house, he saw the Holy Spirit fall on the uncircumcised Gentiles, heard them speak in tongues, as the apostles did on Pentecost, and went as far as to authorize their baptism (see Acts 10 and 11). For all we know, from that moment until the time Paul speaks of in Antioch, Peter ate with Gentiles whenever the occasion demanded. That is why Paul would write:

> Gal. 2:14. ...I said to Peter before them all, "If you, being
> a Jew, live in the manner of Gentiles and not as the Jews,
> why do you compel Gentiles to live as Jews?"

This provokes Paul to call Peter a hypocrite in public!
Peter's change had something to do with **certain men [who] came from James** (v. 12). This was James, the brother of Jesus, who by then had assumed his position as the leader of the Jerusalem church. The apostles had by then begun their itinerant ministries and had given the church's responsibilities to the elders, one of whom was James.
Sometimes we are hesitant to believe that those believers, in what we often consider a model church in Jerusalem, were so ethnocentric, not to say racist. We would like to believe that the circumcision party, which taught that Gentiles had to make a racial decision to become Jews in order to be saved, was a tiny

minority among the believers in Jerusalem. No concrete indications show such was the case. Just the contrary. If these Judaizers
came from James, they were sent by what we would call today
the senior pastor.

The Judaizers would have met with Peter in the Jewish quarter of Antioch, where they would have lodged, and would have
been circulating among the house churches of Messianic believers and the synagogues on the Sabbath. They would have said
something to this effect: "Brother Peter, you are a very influential person. We in Jerusalem see you as the top leader of the
whole Jesus movement. When you were in Jerusalem with us you
ate kosher food. But since you have come here to Antioch we
know that you have visited so-called Gentile believers on the
other side of town. You have not only participated in worship in
Gentiles' houses, but we hear that you even sit down and eat
with them. Don't you realize that this is controversial? Don't you
realize that this can divide the Body of Christ? Some of the young
believers have stumbled in their faith because of this. The church
is confused. James and the other elders have sent us to help you
see the harmful consequences of your behavior and encourage
you to remain a true Jew as we are."

Whether this was the way the dialogue actually went or not,
Peter was persuaded to change. He withdrew and separated himself [from the Gentiles], fearing those who were of the circumcision (v. 12).

This was the root of the conflict between Paul and Peter. But
each one brought to the situation an important personal viewpoint based on their respective prophetic callings.

The Prophetic Calling

Those who are familiar with Campus Crusade for Christ know
that the first of the "four spiritual laws" is: "God loves you and

has a wonderful plan for your life." The first part of fulfilling that wonderful plan is to bring a person into fellowship with God through Jesus Christ.

The second part of the plan of God for each person is to form him or her into a specific member of the Body of Christ through spiritual gifts, and then assign them to a specific ministry in the kingdom of God. This assignment is sometimes called a "prophetic calling." The word "prophetic" refers to the source of the calling, not the resultant ministry. The source is God and prophecy connotes divine-human communication. I can be secure in my calling to the degree that I am convinced it has come directly from God and is God's will for my life.

Notice how Paul referred back to such prophecy when he wrote to Timothy: "This charge I commit to you, son Timothy, according to the prophecies previously made concerning you" (1 Tim. 1:18). Both Paul and Timothy could agree on the direction Timothy was to take because they were convinced it was God's will for his life, not some human plan.

The prophetic calling can come through a recognized prophet. It also can be a direct word from the Lord, as Paul experienced on the Damascus road. It can be an angel, as was the announcement to Mary that she would be the mother of Jesus. It can come through a group of leaders or prayer partners, which may have been Timothy's case: "Do not neglect the gift that is in you, which was given to you by prophecy with the laying on of the hands of the presbytery" (4:14). Or it can come in any number of other ways. We know how Paul received his calling, for example, but we do not have similar information concerning Peter.

Peter's Lose-Lose Predicament

The major point is that Paul and Peter each had received prophetic callings that were similar but also significantly different. Paul was called to be an apostle to the *Gentiles*; Peter was called to be an apostle to the *Jews*. Here is what Paul says:

> Gal. 2:7. ...the gospel for the uncircumcised had been committed to me, as the gospel for the circumcised was to Peter 8. (for He who worked effectively in Peter for the apostleship to the circumcised also worked effectively in me toward the Gentiles).

Being sure of a prophetic calling is an important factor in any Christian leader's decision-making process. Unfortunately, many times a decision must be made in the context of a lose-lose situation. Some refer to this as "between a rock and a hard place." No one likes to be forced to make a choice that cannot avoid offending some people, but Peter had been caught in such a predicament. The question was not whether his decision about eating with Gentiles would offend someone. The question was: Whom would he choose to offend?

In Antioch, Peter's decision would inevitably offend either Paul and the Gentile believers or James and the Jewish believers. When seen in that light, the choice for Peter would have been painful, but not difficult. Peter's prophetic calling was **the apostleship to the circumcised** (v. 8). He, therefore, felt he had to take the side of the Jews and no longer eat with the Gentiles.

Paul's Point of View

Predictably, Peter's decision irritated Paul immensely. He uses extremely strong language. **I withstood him to his face, because he was to be blamed** (v. 11). He labels Peter a hypocrite. These accusations were not made discretely behind closed doors, but they were made in public: **I said to Peter before them all** (v. 14). This was not a small thing to Paul because the very life and death of his evangelistic ministry to the Gentiles was at stake. The Judaizers were undermining the doctrine of justification by faith. Paul was speaking from his prophetic calling as an apostle to the uncircumcision. Paul had declared, "by Him [Jesus Christ] everyone who believes is justified from all things from which you could not be justified by the law of Moses" (Acts 13:39). Peter's friends in the Jerusalem church still strongly disagreed.

We have details on Paul's side of the story only. Because of this, many Bible students are understandably biased toward supporting Paul and condemning Peter for his actions. We also tend to be biased toward Paul because his doctrine of justification by faith apart from the law rightly has prevailed throughout Christian history. However, the conflict between Paul and Peter was not essentially a theological conflict. Peter had learned the rudiments of the theology of justification by faith not only from being with Jesus, but also while visiting the house of Cornelius. He asserted it publicly at the Council of Jerusalem, which was soon to be convened. The issue was not so much theological as behavioral. Let's try to reconstruct Peter's point of view.

Peter's Point of View

The church in Jerusalem was in a critical point at this particular time, A.D. 48. The first wave of persecution had come in A.D. 32 following Stephen's speech. As we have seen, this persecution was directed against the Hellenistic Jews who had emigrated to Jerusalem from all over the Roman Empire. The Hebrew Jews, natives of Jerusalem, were exempted from the persecution.

Peace then reigned in Jerusalem for several years until Peter went to Cornelius's house in A.D. 40 and authorized the baptism of uncircumcised Gentiles. The apostles and Jerusalem church leaders cautiously accepted Peter's explanation, and apparently this incident that took place in distant Caesarea did not provoke particularly serious problems among the believers themselves. As the word got out to the *unbelieving* Jews in Jerusalem, however, they became upset with Peter and the other apostles. In A.D. 42, King Herod took advantage of this tension and for political reasons initiated a new persecution, this time against the apostles. Herod killed the apostle James and almost succeeded in killing Peter. This pleased the Jews (see Acts 12:3).

Herod died two years later in A.D. 44, and following that the gospel spread rapidly among the Jews, much to the displeasure of the establishment. During the years after Herod's death some of the Jewish Zealots, who were advocating a declaration of independence from Rome, had become influential in the political sphere. Meanwhile, the Hellenistic missionaries from Cyprus and Cyrene had gone to Antioch in A.D. 45 and planted Gentile churches for the first time. The believers in Jerusalem had sent Barnabas, desiring to establish cordial relationships with them. This provoked new harassment from the unbelieving Zealots in Jerusalem, who accused the believers of being soft on Gentiles.

During this time, the apostles had begun moving out in their itinerant ministries, leaving the Jerusalem church in the hands of the elders, chief among whom was James, the brother of Jesus. From what we see in Galatians, James was by then leaning toward the stricter position on the circumcision of Gentile believers.

By the time of the overt disagreement between Paul and Peter in A.D. 48, James and the other church leaders had been emotionally worn down by the constant harassment they had been receiving. Understandably, they wanted peace as much as anything else. James apparently had sent a message to Peter that his behavior in Antioch was causing unnecessary turmoil in Jerusalem. Peter, feeling the emotional effects of harassment himself, decided that preserving the peace of the Jerusalem church needed to be his highest priority at the moment so he agreed to change his behavior.

This hypothetical reconstruction of the situation from Peter's point of view is not to excuse Peter for failing to live according to the doctrine he believed. Perhaps Paul was accurate in accusing him of hypocrisy. But at the same time, it may help us sympathize with some of the agony behind Peter's difficult decision.

The Church of Jesus Christ, through 2,000 years of history, has gone through many turmoils similar to the one that was taking place in the four years from A.D. 45 through A.D. 48. As I have said, the issue of Gentile circumcision is by all measurements one of the most crucial missiological challenges in the entire history of Christianity. We should not be surprised that some of the decisions that were made under such circumstances might have been unwise, and that some of the language used might have been harsher than intended. Thankfully, and to the glory of God, the disputes were responsibly dealt with and finally resolved in the approaching Council of Jerusalem.

The Epistle to the Galatians is Paul's personal response to these tumultuous events, previous to the Jerusalem Council. It is important to keep in mind that in his letter, Paul was addressing the Gentile churches he had planted during his first term as a missionary. He was not writing to the Messianic Jews in Jerusalem. By writing to these churches, he was thereby fulfilling his prophetic calling. As he later said to King Agrippa, "I was not disobedient to the heavenly vision" (Acts 26:19).

Galatians in a Nutshell

Paul writes his first epistle in the midst of missiological turmoil. He is in the heart of a controversy of enormous importance. After the briefest of a formal salutation, he immediately raises the issue at hand:

> Gal. 1:6. I marvel that you are turning away so soon from Him who called you in the grace of Christ, to a different gospel, 7. which is not another; but there are some who trouble you and want to pervert the gospel of Christ.

Keeping in mind that the Judaizers had followed his trail and had tried to discredit his theology, Paul finds it necessary to establish his superior credentials as an apostle. He does this from the middle of Galatians 1 through all of chapter 2. Among other things, he mentions that the original apostles in Jerusalem had agreed with his prophetic calling to be an apostle to the Gentiles:

> Gal. 2:9. And when James, Cephas [Peter], and John, who seemed to be pillars, perceived the grace that had been given to me, they gave me and Barnabas the right hand of fellowship, that we should go to the Gentiles and they to the circumcised.

As he wrote this, Paul must have felt serious frustration in realizing that the three apostles he mentioned, the late James, Peter and John had later turned the Jerusalem church over to the elders under a different James, and that it was from there that these trouble-making Judaizers had come.

Having laid this foundation, Paul gets to the heart of his message and deals with the major problems arising from each of the two groups of people in the churches he had planted:

• Chapter 3 deals with the problems arising from those of the synagogue communities, namely the Jews and former Gentile proselytes.

• Chapter 4 deals with problems arising from pagan Gentiles, including the God-fearers.

• Chapter 5 shows that both of the problems can lead to the works of the flesh as opposed to the fruit of the Spirit.

• Chapter 6 concludes with a personal note.

The Jewish Problem: The Law

The God the Jews worshiped was Jehovah, the true God. For their whole lifetimes, and through generations in the past, they had been taught that God's will for them was to obey the Mosaic law. Paul and Barnabas had taught them that things changed when God sent His Son, Jesus, as the long-awaited Messiah. Jesus brought a new covenant that did not destroy the law, but fulfilled it. Because Jesus died, however, the law was no longer a prerequisite for salvation.

As Messianic Jewish believers, they would have continued to keep the law. It was part of their native culture, given to them by God. But when they were born again they had understood that they were no longer saved by keeping the law, but by faith in Jesus Christ. The believing Jews had accepted this while Paul and Barnabas were there. But when the missionaries left and the Judaizers came they began to change their minds and go back to the false doctrine that if they didn't keep the law they couldn't please God. This was so serious that Paul tells them they had been **bewitched.**

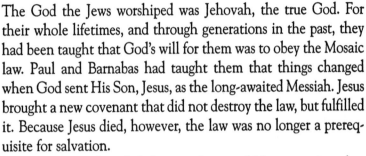

Gal. 3:1. O foolish Galatians! Who has bewitched you that you should not obey the truth, before whose eyes Jesus Christ was clearly portrayed among you as crucified? 2. This only I want to learn from you: Did you receive the Spirit by the works of the law, or by the hearing of faith? 3. Are you so foolish? Having begun in the Spirit, are you now being made perfect by the flesh?

The word **bewitched** from the Greek *baskaino* is a term that was used in the world of magic and the occult. The *New International Dictionary of New Testament Theology* says, "The meaning is to cast a spell by what is called the evil eye."[3] As F. F. Bruce explains, "Their new behavior was so strange, so completely at odds with the liberating message which they had previously accepted, that it appeared as if someone had put a spell on them."[4] This raised the possibility that these Judaizers who were going through the churches were not simply misguided and benign members of the Jerusalem church, but rather, they were perhaps cleverly disguised enemy agents empowered by Satan himself in an effort to abort the fulfillment of Jesus' Great Commission.

If the Judaizers were demonized, the powerful curses they could have placed on these young believers could have subjected them once again to the law. Paul says:

Gal. 3:10. For as many as are of the works of the law are under the curse; for it is written, "Cursed is everyone who does not continue in all things which are written in the book of the law, to do them." 11. But that no one is justified by the law in the sight of God is evident, for "The just shall live by faith."

What is wrong with the law? If you expect to get to God through the law, you depend on human works and not faith. You depend on yourself for salvation, not God.

The Gentile Problem: Evil Spirits

The Gentiles had not previously been in bondage to the law. The major reason the God-fearers of the synagogue communities had not taken the step of becoming Jewish proselytes was that they did not want to submit to the law of Moses. The pain of circumcision was not the major deterrent, as some suppose. Much greater was the pain of inevitable social separation from their Gentile friends and relatives, because the law, as it was then being interpreted, would not allow them to marry or eat with other Gentiles.

The Gentiles had been under a different bondage, that of the principalities and powers of an animistic culture. Paul puts it this way to them:

> **Gal. 4:3. Even so we [Jews], when we were children, were in bondage under the elements of the world.**

And later:

> **Gal. 4:8. But then, indeed, when you did not know God, you served those which by nature are not gods. 9. But now after you have known God, or rather are known by God, how is it that you turn again to the weak and beggarly elements, to which you desire again to be in bondage? 10. You observe days and months and seasons and years.**

The **elements** Paul mentions both in verse 3 and verse 9 is a translation of the Greek *stoicheia*. Kenneth Wuest says that this important word "refers to any first thing from which the others belonging to some series or composite whole take their rise. The word refers to first principles."[5]

Because Paul includes himself as also being under these **elements** in verse 3, it probably has a dual meaning: the original bondage of the *law* for Paul as a Jew, and the original bondage of the *spirit world* for the Gentiles. But then he becomes much more specific in verse 8 when he uses *stoicheia* in the context of **those which by nature are not gods**, referring explicitly to demonic spirits; and he also says in verse 10, **You observe days and months and seasons and years**, which means the occult horoscope and all affiliated with the pagan world of darkness. In other words, one of the dangers for the Gentiles in the churches of Galatia was to turn back to idolatry and yield to what missiologists call "dual allegiance."

In the last chapter, I pointed out that Paul's primary focus in preaching to the Gentiles in Lystra was an "allegiance encounter." Would they turn from Zeus and Hermes as former lords of their lives to Jesus Christ as their only Lord? The major question in their minds was whether Jesus had more power, and the healing of the lame man made it clear to anyone who wished to see that He indeed did.

An extremely common temptation among converts from animism is to cover all their bets and in times of crisis to draw on the powers of the demonic spirits while trying also to live a good Christian life. Missiologist Dean Gilliland tells of an unfortunate event during his ministry in Nigeria in which a pastor's wife was demonized, but neither the missionaries nor the other Nigerian church leaders could help her. The distraught pastor then took the only other recourse he could think of and consulted a witch doctor. Gilliland says, "It was sad to realize that here was a pastor whose desperation had brought him to trust again in 'those weak and pitiful ruling spirits,'"[6] in other words, the *stoicheia*.

Walking in the Spirit

The Jewish believers in Galatia were in danger of allowing *the law* to substitute for the Spirit. The Gentile believers were in danger of allowing *demons* to substitute for the Spirit. Paul writes to them:

> **Gal. 5:16.** I say then: Walk in the Spirit, and you shall not fulfill the lust of the flesh.

There are some objective ways to evaluate whether a person is walking in the Spirit or fulfilling the lust of the flesh.

> **Gal. 5:19.** Now the works of the flesh are....
> **Gal. 5:22.** But the fruit of the Spirit is....

Dependence on the **elements of the world** (4:3), whether they take the form of the law of Moses or the principalities of darkness, will produce **works of the flesh.** Faith in Jesus Christ will, by His grace, produce **the fruit of the Spirit.**

On to the Council

In instructing the believers in Galatia on holiness in their Christian lives, Paul is not forgetting the implications that the teaching of his enemies, the Judaizers, could have on future Gentile evangelism. To make circumcision a prerequisite for salvation would seal off the gospel from the unreached Gentiles. That is why he says:

> **Gal. 5:2.** Indeed, I Paul, say to you that if you become circumcised, Christ will profit you nothing. **3.** And I testify again to every man who becomes circumcised that he is a debtor to keep the whole law.

An implication here is that some of the Gentile believers were not only in danger of going back to **those which by nature are not gods** (4:8), but amazingly the Judaizers might have been so strongly empowered by demonic forces that they were persuading

Gentile Christians to consider circumcision. This never would have happened if Paul himself had been there in Antioch or Iconium or Lystra or Derbe. That is why Paul writes:

Gal. 4:19. My little children, for whom I labor in birth again until Christ is formed in you, 20. I would like to be present with you....

We can safely assume that when the Judaizers had gone to Antioch of Syria, they were unsuccessful in deviating the Gentile Christians there because Paul was in fact present. Paul's confrontation with the circumcision party, his public rebuke of Peter, and his writing the letter to the Galatians did not in themselves bring closure to the matters related to Gentile conversion. But these things did help to prepare Paul for the momentous summit meeting of first-century Christian leaders, the Council of Jerusalem, which Luke records in Acts 15.

Reflection Questions

1. We hold the church in Jerusalem in such high regard that it seems strange to read it was a strongly ethnocentric church. Do you think the attitude of the Judaizers could compare to racism today? yes P 205
2. Paul uses the term "a different gospel" and combats it strongly in his Epistle to the Galatians. "Different" gospels have continued to appear through the years. Can you name some of them? P 207 armstrong new age
3. Explain in your own words why Paul would call Peter a hypocrite in public. If you were Peter, would you have continued to eat with Gentiles? Knowing what I know now yes
4. In Galatians, Paul writes partly to Jewish believers. What is their problem, and what is the solution? P 218

5. Paul also writes partly to Gentile believers. What is their problem, and what is the solution?

Notes

1. Ronald Y. K. Fung, *The Epistle to the Galatians* (Grand Rapids: William B. Eerdmans Publishing Co., 1988), p. 2.
2. Ibid., pp. 7-8.
3. J. Stafford Wright, "Magic, Sorcery, Magi," *The New International Dictionary of New Testament Theology* Vol. 2, ed., Colin Brown (Grand Rapids: Zondervan Publishing House, 1976), p. 559.
4. F. F. Bruce, *The Epistle to the Galatians: A Commentary on the Greek Text* (Grand Rapids: William B. Eerdmans Publishing Co., 1982), p. 148.
5. Kenneth S. Wuest, *Galatians in the Greek New Testament for the English Reader* (Grand Rapids: William B. Eerdmans Publishing Co., 1946), pp. 113-114.
6. Dean S. Gilliland, *Pauline Theology and Mission Practice* (Grand Rapids: Baker Book House, 1983), p. 195.

CHAPTER

8

Acts 15

The Famous Jerusalem Council

The famous Jerusalem Council was convened because of the success of what I call the Cyprus and Cyrene Mission (CCM) in Antioch of Syria, and then because of Paul and Barnabas's first term as cross-cultural missionaries. Had they failed to accomplish their goal of planting a number of Gentile churches, no controversy would have arisen at this time. The missionaries' success precipitates a chain of events that ultimately breaks barriers for all future Christian missions. Jesus commanded His followers to "Go therefore and make disciples of all the nations" (Matt. 28:19). What happens here is essential for that command to be fulfilled.

Contextualization

The central missiological issue is contextualization. A church is established in one of the world's *ethne*, the Greek word for "nations." In obedience to Jesus, cross-cultural missionaries go out from one *ethnos* or nation or people group to another to plant churches. The new people group has its own culture, distinct from the culture of the sending church. At that point, the crucial questions of contextualization arise and need to be dealt with case by case.

In the new cultural context, what aspects of church life will be different? Which theological principles of culture A are non-negotiable and must be maintained in culture B? Which theological principles, on the other hand, need to be reformulated, reworded or refocused to communicate true Christian beliefs to a different people group who have a different worldview? Will any behavioral patterns be different on the mission field? What about music, Bible translations, church government? What is essentially cultural and what is essentially Christian?

My reason for saying these questions must be dealt with case by case is because we have no standard, universal answers to them. But a little thought will show they are the most crucial issues cross-cultural missionaries will confront if their work is going to be everything God wants it to be. Missionaries, through the years, who have ignored these questions or come upon the wrong answers to them, have been frustrated with minimal fruit for their labors. To put it bluntly, missiological ineptitude at the point of applied contextualization can result in lost people not being saved who otherwise would be saved.

When the first missionaries left one people group—the Jews—to plant churches in another cluster of people groups—the Gentiles—no one would have expected them to have anticipated the issues of contextualization. They were not graduates of a School of World Mission. They were pioneers who would have to learn basically through experience, by trial and error. The missionaries who went from Cyprus and Cyrene to the Gentile quarters in the city of Antioch, as well as Paul and Barnabas who evangelized Cyprus and Galatia, were trailblazers. They had no previous models to follow. Later, when we see Paul and Barnabas addressing the Jerusalem Council, we will not hear theological discourses, but rather reports of their practical missionary experience.

Faulty Contextualization

....

15:1. And certain men came down [to Antioch] from Judea and taught the brethren, "Unless you are circumcised according to the custom of Moses, you cannot be saved."

....

This is the most blatant example of faulty contextualization recorded in the New Testament. In the last chapter, we looked at a detailed description of these Judaizers and their activities. Humanly speaking, their problem is that they were culturally bound. Questions of contextualization had not occurred to them. They assumed that good Christians in Lystra would think like and act like good Christians in Jerusalem. Those who would follow the Judaizers' lead have been all too frequent throughout the history of Christian missions. Many missionaries have uncritically superimposed their own, highly culture-bound form of Christianity on converts in other cultures, never aware of the fundamental damage they might be doing. Most were goodhearted saints of God, although they were poor missiologists.

Paul's first confrontation with such inept missiologists came in Antioch. Not having worked through the relationships of Christianity to culture, they reflected the thinking of most Jewish believers of the day who, as missiologist Paul Pierson says, "assumed that of course pagans would be required to adopt their culture (which they believed to be superior) when they became followers of the Messiah."[1] Paul and Barnabas were incensed:

> 2. Therefore, when Paul and Barnabas had no small dis-
> sension and dispute with them, they determined that Paul
> and Barnabas and certain others of them should go up to
> Jerusalem, to the apostles and elders, about this question.

The confrontation described as no small dissension and dispute took place in Antioch, and rightly so. By then Antioch
would have had the largest network of Gentile house churches of
any place in the world. Why could the dissension not have been
resolved in Antioch?

Help! Call a Summit Meeting!

For one thing, the dissension could not have been resolved in
Antioch because the magnitude of the issues involved required a
summit meeting where the consensus of the supreme leaders of
the Christian movement could be attained. Ernst Haenchen
reflects the virtually unanimous opinion of scholars when he
says, "Chapter 15 [of Acts] is the turning point...the episode
which rounds off and justifies the past developments, and makes
those to come intrinsically possible."[2] Nothing less than the
future unity of the Body of Christ was at stake here. F. F. Bruce
says, "There was a grave danger of a complete cleavage between
the churches of Jerusalem and Judea on the one hand and the
church of Antioch and her daughter-churches on the other."[3]
This matter of whether the contextualization of the gospel could
vary from people group to people group had to be resolved with
the utmost clarity.

The church at Jerusalem, formed 10 days after Jesus' ascension
into heaven on the Day of Pentecost, was then, and always will
be, the mother church of the entire Christian movement. In A.D.

48, this was still a functional, not just honorific, title. It would not be the title much longer. After the Council of Jerusalem, Ernst Haenchen says, "The only significance of Jerusalem for the further destiny of the Church is as a place of sacred memories."[4]

Having said that, there may be another less obvious, but equally plausible, reason the debate on Gentile conversion had to be taken from Antioch to Jerusalem. It comes from Luke's statement that **[the Judaizers] determined that Paul and Barnabas and certain others of them should go up to Jerusalem.** Consider the possibility that Paul and Barnabas were actually winning the debate in Antioch. Suppose the delegates of the circumcision party who were representing their colleagues in Jerusalem were indeed being persuaded that they were wrong? What if they were beginning to have serious doubts about whether Gentiles really needed to be circumcised to be saved?

If such were the case, the fact that the Judaizers were the ones who decided to take the discussion to Jerusalem would be easy to understand. They did not think they had the ability to return to Jerusalem and repeat to James and the others the persuasive arguments of Paul and Barnabas. They naturally would have said, "Please come back to Jerusalem with us and tell them just what you have told us here." If on the other hand the Judaizers had won the argument, they might have been most content to return to Jerusalem alone and take the credit.

Squeezing In a Deputation Tour

....

3. So, being sent on their way by the church, they passed through Phoenicia and Samaria, describing the conversion of the Gentiles; and they caused great joy to all the brethren.

....

Paul, Barnabas and others started off for Jerusalem **being sent on their way by the church**. It could have been that the networks of house churches in Antioch had some sort of an organizational mechanism through which they could authorize Paul and Barnabas to serve as their official delegates to an ecumenical council. This, however, seems improbable to me. **Being sent on their way** could also be taken to signify the financial backing for the trip was provided through the believers in Antioch, most likely from the house churches in the Gentile quarters of the huge city. Apparently this was the custom, at least it was later when Paul wrote to the house churches in Rome asking them to help pay his way to Spain (see Rom. 15:24).

In chapter 5, when Paul and Barnabas were leaving Antioch for their missionary journey, I argued that they were not sent under the direct authority of the church, but that they were sent out by their mission, the CCM. I explained the structural difference between modalities (congregational structures) and sodalities (mission structures), pointing out that most cross-cultural missionary work throughout history has been done by sodalities. Within this framework I take the view that Paul and Barnabas did not seek or need the *authority* of the Antioch church, as if the authority of the CCM were not enough. However, they certainly would have needed the *support* of the Antioch church, which they received.

Between Antioch and Jerusalem they engaged in what today's missionaries call a "deputation tour." Churches love to have informed missionaries visit because it stimulates their vision for the worldwide Christian movement and keeps them from becoming narrowly parochial. It also helps generate prayer for the missionaries. Personal letters, newsletters, tapes, pictures or videos cannot substitute for a personal visit by the missionaries the church has been praying for or will soon start to pray for, as the case may be.

Keep in mind that as Paul and Barnabas **passed through Phoenicia and Samaria** (Acts 15:3), the churches they visited were not Gentile churches as were the ones they were working with in Antioch. The believers in these churches had been circumcised and were committed to obeying the Mosaic law. In Phoenicia, the churches would have mostly consisted of Hellenistic Jews, and in Samaria mostly Samaritans. The news of **the conversion of the Gentiles** came as good news to them, for **they caused great joy to all the brethren.**

Apparently the theological issue related to Gentile circumcision in Antioch, and other places, was not a particular problem in these churches. Simple believers in local congregations are seldom on the cutting edge of theological disputes. They are more interested in hearing how the gospel, accompanied by power encounters, miracles, resurrections from the dead and other outworkings of power ministries, have transformed the lives of individuals and families. They want news of the expansion of the kingdom of God. Paul and Barnabas were probably exceptional missionary speakers and the net result of their visits was positive and stimulating.

The Debate Starts

....

4. And when they had come to Jerusalem, they were received by the church and the apostles and the elders; and they reported all things that God had done with them. 5. But some of the sect of the Pharisees who believed rose up, saying, "It is necessary to circumcise them, and to command them to keep the law of Moses."

....

When Paul and Barnabas and their entourage arrived in Jerusalem, arrangements had been made for the summit meeting.

The news that Paul and Barnabas had agreed to go to Jerusalem may have reached Jerusalem any number of ways, one possibility being that the Judaizers who had confronted Paul in Antioch had returned directly to Jerusalem while the others were traveling at a slower pace, visiting the churches in Phoenicia and Syria.

They were received by the church and the apostles and the elders. Naturally, the church and the elders would have been there. But the presence of the *apostles* is unusual, if indeed they had by then set out for other places on their itinerant work, as I suspect. Given the difficulties of travel in those days, the presence of some of the apostles in Jerusalem is a convincing indication that the leaders were fully aware of the transcendent significance of the approaching council.

Luke does not choose to emphasize the spiritual activities that must have been associated with such a meeting. Therefore, our collective impressions of these events in books and sermons usually deal with the experiences Paul and Barnabas had on the mission field, the reactionary theology of **the sect of the Pharisees** and the mechanisms of how the Council of Jerusalem was conducted. Although these are of central importance, we must suppose that other gifts of the Holy Spirit were also in operation, such as prophecy and intercession. For example, part of **the church** that received Paul and Barnabas would have been the group of intercessors who met in the house of Mary, the mother of Mark (see 12:12). Knowing the desire of Satan to abort the whole Christian movement at this early stage, the spiritual warfare accompanying the Jerusalem Council must have been intense, and it is not beyond reason to suppose that the frontline engagement with the enemy was taking place in Mary's house.

Paul and Barnabas **reported all things that God had done with them** (15:4). The response to their reports was quite different, however, from that of the churches in Phoenicia and

Samaria. Luke does not say that they caused great joy among the brethren in Jerusalem. Instead, he tells us that some people in the audience directly confronted them, telling them they were wrong! The members of **the sect of the Pharisees** were those who were supposed to know the Bible, which then of course was the Old Testament. They were the ranking theologians, the professionals.

There is little question that these theologians' knowledge of the Bible was accurate. But like any number of theologians today who also know the Bible well, they had failed to tune in to some of the new things God was doing in their midst. They were not hearing what the Spirit was saying to the churches. But they did represent a widespread position among the leaders of the Messianic Jewish movement of the day, namely that non-Jews were not fully acceptable to God and that, therefore, Gentiles could not be saved without first becoming Jews through circumcision.

The results of the Jerusalem Council were not a foregone conclusion. It would not be a simple matter to gain a consensus, among those leaders who had gathered in Jerusalem, that what Paul and Barnabas had been doing and saying would be acceptable to all from now on.

Fortunately, the Pharisee believers, professionals that they were, could not intimidate Paul, who likewise had the credentials of a Pharisee. And few of them, if any, would have had the seniority of a Barnabas who was nothing less than a charter member of the Jerusalem church. The sides seemed evenly matched.

The Council Comes to Order

....

6. So the apostles and elders came together to consider this matter. 7. And when there had been much dispute,....

....

The Jerusalem Council was a meeting of the apostles representing the church at large, the elders of the Jerusalem church and the missionaries and their colleagues from Antioch. The church (v. 4) in general had gathered to hear the missionaries' report previous to the council, but the deliberations on these momentous issues in the council itself were rightly left to the leaders.

Luke doesn't tell us, but I would think that Simon Kistemaker is correct when he suggests that "the council met for many days to discuss the matter at hand."[5] We, of course, do not have a log of all that took place during those days, but Luke summarizes the events by excerpting from three contributions: those of Peter, of Paul and Barnabas, and of James. Peter is regarded as the chief apostle and James is regarded as the chief elder. The missionaries were those on trial, so to speak.

Peter's Theology

7. ...Peter rose up and said to them: "Men and brethren, you know that a good while ago God chose among us, that by my mouth the Gentiles should hear the word of the gospel and believe. 8. So God, who knows the heart, acknowledged them, by giving them the Holy Spirit just as He did to us, 9. and made no distinction between us and them, purifying their hearts by faith."

Peter's *theology* was correct, although Paul had recently scolded him for failing to consistently apply what he knew. Paul had become seriously upset with Peter in Antioch when he decided to stop eating with the Gentile believers (see Gal. 2:11-14) because of the confusion it had caused there on Paul's turf. But now that Paul was in Jerusalem on Peter's turf, I wonder if Paul might not have seen it differently. As I pointed out in the last chapter,

Peter's "Catch 22" decision may have offended Paul and the Gentile believers in Antioch, but it was a strategic decision, taken to avoid confusion and potential division among the Jewish believers in the Jerusalem church under James. Because of that, Paul's opponents in the circumcision party in Jerusalem likely would have regarded Peter as an ally and, therefore, they would have been open to give serious consideration to anything he said.

Peter said the right things. He did not begin with a philosophical discourse, but reminded the council of his experience in the house of Cornelius something like 10 years previously. Peter's theology again was drawn from his experience. God had sent Peter to Cornelius's house in Caesarea, not to prepare him for a lifetime of ministry to Gentiles—because his calling was to be that of an apostle to the circumcision—but essentially to prepare him for this event, the Council of Jerusalem. Not only had Peter taken the unprecedented action of authorizing the baptism of uncircumcised Gentiles in Cornelius's house in obedience to the leading of the Holy Spirit, but he had also immediately returned to Jerusalem and processed these very same issues with the leadership of the Jerusalem church. They were extremely upset at first, but before their discussion was finished they came to agree with Peter and said, **"Then God has also granted to the Gentiles repentance to life"** (Acts 11:18).

Here in the Council of Jerusalem, Peter relied on the same empirical evidence he had cited previously to validate the authenticity of the conversion of the Gentiles, namely that they had spoken in tongues. This is implied in his assertion that **"God, who knows the heart, acknowledged them, by giving them the Holy Spirit just as He did to us"** (15:8). Back in Cornelius's house, Luke reports that **the gift of the Holy Spirit had been poured out on the Gentiles also. For they heard them speak with tongues** (10:45,46).

Peter's Conclusion and Advice

15:10. "Now therefore, why do you test God by putting a
yoke on the neck of the disciples which neither our
fathers nor we were able to bear? 11. But we believe that
through the grace of the Lord Jesus Christ we shall be
saved in the same manner as they."

Peter's conclusion was that the Gentiles did not need to obey the
Mosaic law to be saved. His reference to **putting a yoke on the
neck of the disciples** would have been understood by all present
at the council as a reference to the Jewish law. F. F. Bruce tells us
that in those days a Gentile who was converting to become a
Jewish proselyte "by undertaking to keep the law of Moses, was
said to 'take up the yoke of the kingdom of heaven.'"[6]

Peter goes right to the heart of the matter. If the yoke of the
gospel as presented to them is too heavy to bear, Gentiles will not
be saved. This is not to say that the law is bad. Jewish converts
would be expected to continue to obey the law of Moses to the best
of their ability. Gentile converts also would find much good in the
law of Moses that would contribute to their subsequent sanctification. But the law was not to be a part and parcel of the initial pre-
sentation of the gospel of salvation. This would be to confuse *perfecting* with *discipling*, as some modern missiologists would say.

Donald McGavran, the founder of the church growth movement, puts it this way: "Antigrowth concepts arise from confusing perfecting with discipling."[7] In this, he is reflecting contemporary efforts to load onto the simple gospel of justification
through faith in Jesus Christ any number of ethical demands
favored by a given preacher. I have heard the gospel presented
with caveats such as: If you want to be saved you must stop smoking or you must renounce polygamy or you must be baptized by

immersion or you must give up racial biases, or, in our case in Jerusalem, you must be circumcised. When this approach is used, the gospel does not move out in the way God intended it to.

If Peter, the most influential Christian leader of that day, had not been correct in his views of discipling versus perfecting, or justification versus sanctification, or faith versus works, the expansion of the Christian movement could have halted then and there.

Peter solidified his point by telling his colleagues what they already knew, namely, that Jews could not be saved by the law either because virtually all of them found it impossible to keep. The yoke of the law was something that **"neither our fathers nor we were able to bear."** Because the participants in the Jerusalem Council were all born-again believers in Jesus Christ, they knew in their hearts that they were saved by grace. But even so, many of them had not yet been able to break away from their inbred ethnocentricity.

If any of them had truly kept the law, Paul would have been among them. He says later in Philippians, "If anyone else thinks he may have confidence in the flesh, I more so:...concerning the righteousness which is in the law, blameless" (3:4,6). But suppose he did keep the law? What good would it have done? Looking back as a Christian, Paul counts keeping the law "as rubbish, that I may gain Christ and be found in Him, not having my own righteousness, which is from the law, but that which is through faith in Christ" (3:8,9).

The Missionaries Report Power Evangelism

15:12. Then all the multitude kept silent and listened to Barnabas and Paul declaring how many miracles and wonders God had worked through them among the Gentiles.

Apparently Peter's address had summarized the consensus that the council had reached after perhaps days of debate. The gathering was now ready to listen to the missionaries who had been admitting uncircumcised Gentiles into their churches. No more debate is recorded. In fact, from this point on, Peter drops out of the scene and Luke has nothing more to say about him in the rest of Acts.

Reminding ourselves of the watershed nature of the Jerusalem Council, it might well be that Peter's influence there could be regarded as his major contribution to the kingdom of God. His ministry had many other notable aspects to be sure, but, at least from the viewpoint of missiology, world evangelization and the fulfillment of the Great Commission, nothing Peter did had more far-reaching positive influence than this. He was a true trailblazer for the future spread of the gospel.

Granted that Luke uses a highly abbreviated account of the presentations Barnabas and Paul made to the members of the Council, his choice of **miracles and wonders** as the one theme to record in this historical account is notable. But what else would they have spoken about? Those who needed persuading would not like hearing about the new churches in Antioch, Iconium, Lystra and Derbe, because they were filled with uncircumcised Gentiles. They had already sent Judaizers throughout the area in an attempt to persuade the church leaders they were wrong. They did not need another theological argument, especially from the pro-Gentile faction. Peter, an insider whom they trusted, had established a correct theological foundation.

Directing Attention to God's Power

The best thing Barnabas and Paul could have done would have been to direct the attention of the assembly away from churches, individuals, doctrines or behavior patterns and turn their attention to God and His power. I like the way Kistemaker puts it: "The emphasis does not fall on what Paul and Barnabas did during their missionary journey but on what God did through them."[8] We do not know how long they talked, but it's unfortunate that history did not leave us a complete transcript of what they said. Certainly Acts 13 and 14 is a bare-bones account at best. Not only were **miracles and wonders** done through the apostles in the churches, but after they left, the Holy Spirit continued doing them through the new believers, including through the uncircumcised Gentile disciples. In Galatians, Paul writes to them: "Therefore He who supplies the Spirit to you and works miracles among you" (3:5).

Among many other things, Barnabas and Paul would in all probability have told the Council about:

• The high-level power encounter in West Cyprus. This would have been a spellbinder to hear about Paul going eyeball-to-eyeball with the sorcerer Bar-Jesus in the presence of the proconsul, Sergius Paulus. As Susan Garrett says, "The human combatants Paul and Bar-Jesus in turn represent superhuman figures."[9] Paul is filled with the Holy Spirit while Bar-Jesus is filled with demonic powers of darkness. It is no contest. God demonstrates through Paul that His power is much greater than that of the enemy, and Sergius Paulus is saved (see Acts 13:6-12).

• The **signs and wonders** that were done in Iconium over a **long time.** Here is one place the missionaries might have filled in many details that Luke does not record (14:3).

• The amazing healing of the lame man in Lystra. Although this culture was accustomed to supernatural power, the magnitude of this miracle so exceeded anything they had known that they regarded Paul and Barnabas as incarnations of Hermes and Zeus, and the missionaries, therefore, had to deal with allegiance encounters (see vv. 6-18).

- Paul himself being raised from the dead in Lystra. Back in Antioch of Pisidia, Paul had announced that salvation was by faith in Jesus and not in the works of the law. This so infuriated the unbelieving Jews that they had the authorities sentence him to be executed by stoning. This incident must have impressed some on the Jerusalem Council, because the Pharisees there could have identified personally with the feelings those Jewish leaders would have had. The persecutors caught up to Paul in Lystra and stoned him to death, but through the prayers of the believers Paul was raised from the dead (see vv. 19,20).

James Announces the Verdict

> 13. And after they had become silent, James answered, saying, "Men and brethren, listen to me: 14. Simon has declared how God at the first visited the Gentiles to take out of them a people for His name."

As a reminder, this James was not only the brother of Jesus, but by now he was also the leading elder in the Jerusalem church. He later wrote the Epistle of James and is referred to in history as "James the Just," undoubtedly because he had the spiritual gift of wisdom. James's wisdom was evident here in his concluding message. Notice that he wisely makes no reference to what Barnabas and Paul had said, but instead he refers to Peter's input. Those present who needed an attitude adjustment were those who respected Peter, and suspected Barnabas and Paul.

Apparently James, either during the council or before, had modified his own position. We see from Galatians that the Judaizers who went to Antioch of Syria and precipitated this whole controversy with Paul and Barnabas "came from James" (Gal. 2:12). Another possible explanation is that James might have sympathized with Paul's position from the start. But because he had no personal experience with Gentiles he couldn't persuade the circumcision party so he sent some of them to be persuaded by Paul. James had never eaten with Gentiles, but Paul had. However he arrived at it, James's conclusion now was that "God at the first visited the Gentiles to take out of them a people for His name" (Acts 15:14).

We shouldn't pass this by too rapidly. John Stott says, "[James's] statement is considerably more significant than it looks at first sight."[10] From the time of Abraham until now, the people of God had been chosen from among the Jews. James is now saying that the believing Gentiles, on their own merits, are accepted by God as if they were Israel. Such a statement would have confirmed the worst fears of the hard-core Judaizers present at the council, but no more arguments are recorded. The power of the Holy Spirit over this gathering must have been awesome to bring about such a consensus, although Luke does not mention that factor in his text. I can only speculate that the intercessors in Mary's house were once again winning the spiritual battle through prayer, as they had when Herod was planning to kill Peter.

To nail down his point, James goes immediately to the prophets, in this case Amos 9:11,12:

15:15. "And with this the words of the prophets agree, just as it is written: 16. 'After this I will return and will rebuild the tabernacle of David which has fallen down. I will rebuild its ruins, and I will set it up, 17. so that the rest of mankind may seek the Lord, even all the Gentiles who are called by My name, says the Lord who does all these things.'"

The major point James is attempting to make by citing this

prophecy is that the notion of God's bringing Gentiles into the kingdom as His people was part of His long-range plan, not some precipitous change of plans at the time of sending Peter to Cornelius's house.

It is interesting that James does not quote Amos from the Hebrew Bible, but from the Greek translation called the *Septuagint* or *LXX*. James does this because it makes his point much more forcefully. We should not be surprised at this because many of us do the same thing. If *The Living Bible*, for example, makes our point more clearly than the *New International Version* or the *King James Version*, we usually use *The Living Bible* for that particular matter. Many of the scholarly commentaries discuss this use of the *LXX* in detail, and I recommend these commentaries to those who may be interested.

James's conclusion constitutes the most important missiological statement ever made this side of Pentecost:

19. "Therefore I judge that we should not trouble those from among the Gentiles who are turning to God."

The way is open now for missionaries to take the gospel to every unreached people group in all six continents and to seek God's leading on how the gospel will be contextualized for each one.

Some Diplomatic Concessions

James again exhibits his gift of wisdom by suggesting how this history-making decision can be communicated to the churches while still maintaining the basic unity of the Body of Christ.

20. "But that we write to them [the Gentiles] to abstain from things polluted by idols, from sexual immorality,

from things strangled, and from blood. 21. For Moses has
had throughout many generations those who preach him
in every city, being read in the synagogues every Sabbath."

The letter they wrote read:

23. ...To the brethren who are of the Gentiles in Antioch,
Syria, and Cilicia:....

The first thing the recipients of the letter would have looked
for would have been what it said about circumcision, and much
to their relief this was not made a requirement. They did not
have to become Jews to be saved or to live a good Christian life.
They could remain Gentiles forever. Keeping the law of Moses
was unnecessary either for salvation or for sanctification.

At the same time, because those who had been Judaizers also
deserved to have their opinions heard and reflected in the decisions of the council, some diplomatic concessions were made.
The Gentiles were to be careful about the food they ate, abstain-
ing from meat offered to idols and from strangled meat that still
contained blood, or from the blood itself. They were also to live
lives free from sexual immorality. Why immorality would have
been included in the list of four is not entirely clear, except that
Gentiles were, as a cultural characteristic, much more prone to
immorality than Jews. In most of the New Testament lists of sins
it is on the top of the list. And in many of the pagan cultures, ritual immorality with temple prostitutes was a way of life, encouraged rather than condemned by society.

22. Then it pleased the apostles and elders, with the
whole church, to send chosen men of their own company

to Antioch with Paul and Barnabas, namely, Judas
who was also named Barsabas, and Silas, leading
men among the brethren.

....

We know nothing more about Judas except for this visit to
Antioch. Silas, however, later joins Paul's mission for the next
trip back through the churches of Galatia and beyond.

....

30. So when they were sent off, they came to Antioch;
and when they had gathered the multitude together,
they delivered the letter. 31. When they had read it,
they rejoiced over its encouragement.
32. Now Judas and Silas, themselves being prophets also,
exhorted the brethren with many words and strengthened
them. 33. And after they had stayed there for a time,
they were sent back with greetings from the brethren
to the apostles.
34. However, it seemed good to Silas to remain there.
35. Paul and Barnabas also remained in Antioch, teaching
and preaching the word of the Lord, with many others also.

....

Because the letter asserted that the Gentiles could maintain
their own cultural identity and integrity and still be accepted as
faithful followers of Jesus Christ, the Gentiles **rejoiced over its
encouragement.** The four conditions mentioned in the letter did
not seem to cause any significant negative reactions. Actually,
after Paul had fulfilled his obligation of reading the letter to the
churches he had planted in Asia Minor (see 16:4), he himself did
not seem to follow the guidelines of the dietary decrees. As we
will see, his own later writings indicate this. He, of course, upheld
the standard of sexual morality at all times.

The house churches in Antioch had become accustomed to

having those who had the gift of prophecy circulate among them. The five leaders of the Cyprus and Cyrene Mission were said to be **prophets and teachers** (13:1). Therefore, the prophetic ministry of Judas and Silas was not something unusual for them. Those who have the spiritual gift of prophecy are a great blessing to congregations and also to individual believers because they deliver personal prophecies from the Lord. As Paul later writes, "He who prophesies speaks edification and exhortation and comfort to men" (1 Cor. 14:3). My wife, Doris, and I have been greatly enriched in our spiritual lives and ministries over the years through the ministry of those who have the gift of prophecy, especially among our active team of personal intercessors. We keep a private "Prophetic Journal," preserving those prophecies we regard as particularly significant.

The Reorganization of the CCM

Before Paul leaves for his next missionary trip, a major reorganization of the Cyprus and Cyrene Mission takes place. Because it fits more directly into the events of Acts 16, I will postpone commenting on this reorganization until we begin Paul's second term of service in the next and final book of this series.

Reflection Questions

1. Discuss the meaning of "contextualization." From your knowledge of foreign missions yesterday and today, can you find some examples of mistakes in this area? *P 225-226*
2. The debate about Gentile circumcision erupted in Antioch. Why then, was the summit meeting called in Jerusalem? *P.228*
3. How could it be possible that the highest-ranking theologians in the Jerusalem church, those of the sect of the Pharisees, could miss hearing what the Spirit was saying to the churches? Could the same thing be possible in our times? *P. 233*

4. A key to the positive outcome of the Jerusalem Council was Peter's speech. What parts of Peter's previous experience in the house of Cornelius were crucial in shaping his point of view?
5. Would you think it is an exaggeration to say that the Council of Jerusalem was the most important meeting of the church in all of history? Why or why not?

Notes

1. Paul E. Pierson, *Themes from Acts* (Ventura, CA: Regal Books, 1982), p. 115.
2. Ernst Haenchen, *The Acts of the Apostles* (Philadelphia: The Westminster Press, 1971), p. 461.
3. F. F. Bruce, *The Book of Acts* (Grand Rapids: William B. Eerdmans Publishing Co., 1954; revised edition, 1988), p. 287.
4. Haenchen, *The Acts of the Apostles*, p. 462.
5. Simon J. Kistemaker, *Exposition of the Acts of the Apostles* (Grand Rapids: Baker Book House, 1990), p. 543.
6. Bruce, *The Book of Acts*, p. 290.
7. Donald A. McGavran, *Understanding Church Growth* (Grand Rapids: William B. Eerdmans Publishing Co., 1970; 1980; third edition revised and edited by C. Peter Wagner, 1990), p. 123.
8. Kistemaker, *Exposition of the Acts*, p. 549.
9. Susan R. Garrett, *The Demise of the Devil: Magic and the Demonic in Luke's Writings* (Minneapolis: Fortress Press, 1989), p. 80.
10. John Stott, *The Spirit, the Church and the World: The Message of Acts* (Downers Grove, IL: InterVarsity Press, 1990), p. 247.

INDEX

....

More Resources to Move Your Church to Action